THE LAND OF OLD RENOWN

'THE LAND OF OLD RENOWN'

George Borrow in North Wales

Dewi Roberts

Text © Dewi Roberts 1997

ISBN: 0-86381-436-0

Cover: Alan Jones
Map: Ken Gruffydd

First published in 1997 by Gwasg Carreg Gwalch,
12 Iard yr Orsaf, Llanrwst, Conwy, Wales.
☎ (01492) 642031

Printed and Published in Wales

For Ian Skidmore

I am indebted to the following for permission to quote from works which they have published:

Seren Books *for the poem* Yr Wyddfa Speaks Out *and one verse from* Yn y Carchar *which are taken from* This House, My Ghetto *by Mike Jenkins.*

The WEA *for two verses from* The New Welsh Bible *by James Nicholas, translated by Tony Conran.*

I also wish to offer thanks to my publisher, Myrddin ap Dafydd, who responded so enthusiastically when I put the idea for this book to him.

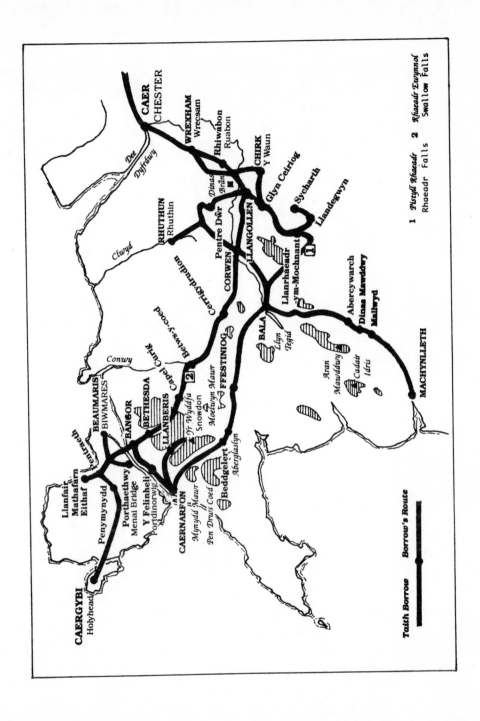

CONTENTS

INTRODUCTION

Within the last century George Borrow's 'Wild Wales' has enjoyed an enduring popularity unrivalled by other travel books about Wales. Published in 1862, it describes his experiences in and impressions of the country during a series of pedestrian tours eight years earlier, in 1854. For all their merits the accounts of previous literary tourists are not comparable to Borrow's contribution, and this is largely due to the inherent limitations of the tourists themselves, their lack of any previous knowledge of the country and its people and the difficulty of communicating with a native population with, very often, no real knowledge of the English language.

Borrow, on the contrary, was able to actually speak the language and had read and digested the works of a number of the national poets. He was eager to seek out places with which certain of these writers were associated and, in describing encounters on his journeys, uses a good deal of dialogue which enables us to obtain a much clearer impression of the Welsh than would have been the case otherwise.

But who was George Borrow and what was his background? He was born in East Dereham in Norfolk in 1803 the son of an army recruiting officer. Of necessity, therefore, his youth was one in which he moved around quite a lot as his father attempted to gain support for the kings' cause. From an early age he developed a flair for languages. He learned some Latin and Greek while at school, some Irish while he was in that country, and later, while being briefly in the employment of a solicitor in Norwich, Welsh. This he was able to do partly from books, including a Welsh translation of Milton's 'Paradise Lost', and also from a groom who worked close to the legal practice. The groom was treated rather unkindly by Borrow's fellow clerks. They reproached his Welshness and would chant in his hearing:

'Taffy was a Welshman
Taffy was a thief.'

11

Borrow did not join in, for as he writes:

> 'I was trying to learn Welsh and the idea occuring to me that the groom might be able to assist me in my pursuit, I instantly lost all desire to torment him and determined to do my best to scrape acquaintance with him and persuade him to give me what assistance he could.'

Within the next few years he was also able to learn Danish, French, Italian, Spanish and Portuguese. He also became intensely interested in the life and culture of the Gypsies whose language he had also mastered; so much so, in fact, that he was able to compile a Gypsy dictionary. He was engaged as a travelling agent of the Bible Society and this took him to Spain. His remarkable account of that country is contained in 'The Bible in Spain' published in 1843, which was an instant success, making him as famous at that time as Dickens and Thackeray. But such are the fluctuations of literary taste that the two subsequent books, 'Lavengro' and 'The Romany Rye', met with a dismal response. 'Wild Wales' was only moderately successful. For the remaining years of his long life – he died in 1881 – Borrow became virtually a forgotten figure.

But at the beginning of our own century came a wave of interest in the book, and in Borrow's other writings as well. It was the beginning of the era of tourism as we know it today and people from urban areas were seeking the solitude and scenic beauty of the countryside both on foot and on bicycles. 'Wild Wales' somehow caught the romantic imagination and the word Borrovian found its way into the literary vocabulary.

But the book is not only about Wales, for Borrow reveals a good deal about himself in every chapter. A Low Church Anglican he beat the anti-Popery drum whenever the opportunity arose, and was racially intolerant, as his encounter with a coloured man at Chester reveals. He was capable of considerable egotism and tended to flaunt his linguistic superiority at times and was capable of prolonging a misunderstanding. But he was a genuine scholar with a passion for out-of-the-way knowledge. Physically he was formidable, and often walked between twenty and thirty miles a day. Mind you, he fuelled himself with some very large breakfasts. At Bala, for example, he went down to:

> '...pot of hare; ditto of trout; pot of prepared shrimps; tin of sardines; beautiful beef steak; eggs, muffin; large loaf, and butter, not forgetting capital tea.'

Today many hikers make do with cornflakes and a round of toast, but then they don't trek thirty miles to recite the poetry of Goronwy Owen from the top of Snowdon!

He was fifty six when he undertook his journeys. Having travelled to Chester with his wife and stepdaughter from their home in Yarmouth he left them there and continued on foot over the border into Wales arriving at Llangollen on 1st August. His family joined him there and they stayed at Dee Cottage. Initially he was content to make excursions to places within fairly easy reach of the town, Ruthin and Valle Crucis Abbey included. But he wished to achieve his object in coming to Wales and later made the journey to Bangor. He used Bangor as a further excursion centre and went up Snowdon, to Anglesey, and returned to Llangollen via Beddgelert, Ffestiniog and Bala. He then spent more time with his family there before leaving them in order to make the long journey to South Wales.

'Wild Wales' is a long book, but Borrow devotes considerably more space to North Wales than he does to mid and South Wales. In writing this book, therefore, I felt that to write about some of the places which he visited in the North, and to attempt to reveal the changes which have come about since 1854, would present a sufficiently challenging task, and that, possibly, the South Wales journey might be explored by someone in a separate volume. Having said this, however, one has to admit that his comments on the North are, in general, more interesting, partly because of the literary associations which he wished to know more about. What Borrow has to say about Llangollen alone – and he has substantially more to say about this town than any other town in Wales – is of the greatest interest.

The changes since Borrow's time have been enormous. Roads were extremely primitive when compared with the roads of today, although the Holyhead Road, or the A5 as we know it today, had been improved prior to Borrow's visit, in order to facilitate stage coach travel. Nowadays, of course, motorised traffic travels at high speed along this road, a route which, together with the A55, has really opened up Wales to visitors. It comes as no surprise to learn that tourism in the country currently employs 80,000 people.

Although the topography of North Wales offers a great deal in terms of natural beauty there are certain features which have created acrimony.

Windfarms provide an alternative form of power, but their presence has incurred the wrath of some who claim that they are an eye sore. (The largest in Europe is situated in mid-Wales). The Forestry Commission have planted thousands of acres of conifers throughout Wales, whereas

Borrow would have seen only the traditional woodlands of oak, birch, hawthorn, sycamore and so forth which are, mercifully, still found in older woodland areas today. And then there are the unequivocal blots on the landscape: camping and caravan sites in scenically sensitive areas and ever expanding housing development which has been given the go ahead by uncaring 'public servants'.

Almost every Welsh town has changed vastly within a matter of decades – including the one in which I live-and all communities now face the problems of crime, drug dependency, unemployment, vandalism, and a glance at any local newspaper will confirm this, if confirmation is needed. A few years ago one of the towns which figures in this book, Holyhead, was dubbed the most depressed town in Britain.

So, up to a point, 'Wild Wales' may be seen as an evocation of the country as it was before the Fall, before all the singular disadvantages of life today. But, in my view, it is not a book which creates nostalgia in the reader for a time which he or she never knew, for, as history has related, the life of the common people in Victorian times was hardly a bed of roses!

I should add at this point that I am now exactly the same age as Borrow was when he undertook his walks in the

'...land of old renown and of wonder'.

But, unlike him, I have to admit that I have travelled by car over large stretches of the region. Imagine how the old boy would disapprove of that! It would be virtually impossible to retrace his exact footsteps with any degree of pleasure today, and, one would be forced to stride down the A5 amid the roar and fumes of passing traffic.

I write as a Borrovian enthusiast and there will be many times in the following pages when I shall be making apt digressions and expressing personal opinions. I make no apology for this, for this is a travel book and a bland work in this genre would soon make dull reading.

Dewi Roberts,
Denbigh.

Chapter One

CHESTER AND WREXHAM: BOTH SIDES OF THE BORDER

'With dragon speed, and dragon noise, fire smoke, and fury, the train dashed along its road through beautiful meadows...Quite forgetting everything Welsh, I was enthusiastically Saxon the whole way from Medeshamsted to Blissworth, so thoroughly Saxon was the country, with its rich meads, its old churches and its names.'

This is a part of George Borrow's lively account of an early stage in his journey from his home in Norfolk to Chester, and ultimately to Wales. There are times in 'Wild Wales' when he reveals himself as a national chauvinist, although there are a number of instances where he becomes so utterly impressed by things Welsh that he is quite prepared to be critical of his own race. For a man who had such strong, sometimes objectionable, prejudices, in other respects, this may be regarded as a fairly unlikely quality in Borrow. But it does illustrate at least something about the complexity of the man.

But to return to that important train journey, which now takes us into the border country:

'I sat silent and melancholy, till looking from the window I caught sight of a long line of hills, which I guessed to be the Welsh hills, which sight caused me to remember that I was bound for Wales, the land of the bard, which thought made me cast all gloomy thoughts aside and glow with all the Welsh enthusiasm with which I glowed when I first started in the direction of Wales.'

On their arrival in Chester he and his wife and step-daughter found accommodation in Northgate Street. He ordered tea for his family and ale for himself. This he found of better quality than the ale written about by Siôn Tudur, whom he quotes:

> 'Chester ale, Chester ale! I could ne'r get it down,
>   Tis made of ground ivy, of dirt and of bran,
> Tis as thick as a river below a huge town!
> Tis not lap for a dog, far less drink for a man.'

The family spent a matter of days in Chester and during that time Borrow took the opportunity to walk on the city walls. From here he was able to gaze out towards the hills of North-East Wales.

He also encountered a coloured man, with whom he got into conversation. The man told Borrow that he was sold as a slave at an earlier period of his life, and when he obtained his freedom he was engaged by an English gentleman as his servant. But he disliked the work and left. Since then he had spoken out against slavery at religious meetings, but did not feel inclined to work in any other way.

> 'I asked him if he knew anything about the Americans? He said he did, and that they were very bad people who kept slaves and flogged them.
> 'And quite right too,' said I, 'if they are lazy rascals like yourself, who want to eat without working. What a pretty set of knaves or fools must they be, who encourage a fellow like you to speak against Negro slavery...'

This must be one of the most overtly racist passages in the whole of Victorian literature, and one could even understand certain readers abandoning the book at this stage in disgust.

Further evidence of Borrow's downright arrogance and intolerance is contained within the same chapter: He describes a Sunday morning visit to an open air religious meeting where

> '...two thousand people gathered together in a field near the railway station.'

The speaker is promoting the immorality of drinking. A man standing close to Borrow is critical of the speaker:

> 'It was only the other day I saw him reeling out of a gin-shop?'
> Now that speech I did not like, for I saw at once that it could not be

true, so I turned round and said:

'Old chap, I can scarcely credit that!'

The man whom I addressed, a rough-and-ready looking fellow of the lower class, seemed half disposed to return me a savage answer; but an Englishman of the lower class, though you can call his word in question, is never savage with you provided you call him old chap and he considers you by your dress to be superior in station.'

This is a very good example of Borrow's apparent need to elevate himself above many of the people he conversed with; he clearly regarded himself as superior to them. Often the indications of this are fairly subtle and the way in which he is careful to record the way in which people address him in conversation is another manifestation of this. Many address him as 'sir' or 'your honour' and one can't help feeling that this is a fillip to Borrow's ego.

Borrow's most obviously negative characteristic is his condescension. In parting from a Cheshire man whom he has been chatting to in the streets of Chester he exclaims:

'You are a noble fellow and a credit to Cheshire. Will you have sixpence to drink?'

'Thank you, Measter, I shall stop at Pulford and shall be glad to drink your health in a jugful of ale.'

Borrow, like Dickens his contemporary, had a considerable sense of the dramatic and one can hear the dialogue being spoken. But in calling the man a 'noble fellow' and giving him sixpence one cannot help feeling that he was again attempting to gratify some ego need.

On an evening walk through Chester Borrow discovered that

'...the streets were crowded with people, many of whom must have been Welsh, as I heard the Cambrian language spoken on every side.'

You will still hear a certain amount of Welsh spoken in the streets of the city, but you will also hear a blend of many other accents, especially during the Summer months: the native accents of foreign tourists, Scouse, standard English, and North country.

Chester is an affluent city, comfortably middle-class, with a considerable sense of civic pride.

* * *

'It is a stirring, bustling place of much traffic and of several thousand inhabitants.'

writes Borrow of Wrexham, through which he travelled on his way to Llangollen.

This is still an apt description of the town, although the thousands have been added to since Victorian times and, if anything, it bustles even more today.

Although our veteran traveller does not actually refer to Wrexham's close proximity to the English border he does hint at the result of this geographical proximity when he goes on to describe it as

'...a Welsh town, but its appearance is not Welsh – its inhabitants have neither the look nor language of Welshmen.'

He was also told that little Welsh was spoken by the townspeople, and this must surely be the case today. The accent of the people of the area is distinct and I have always thought that it is very similar to that to be found in the area once covered by the old county of Montgomeryshire.

Borrow was much impressed by St Giles' Church, the steeple of which is one of the seven wonders of Wales. It is certainly one of the finest religious buildings in Wales, and the construction of it is a living testimony to the immensely strong spiritual faith of earlier generations.

In the churchyard Borrow failed to observe the grave of Elihu Yale, who was the generous benefactor of the college in Connecticut which bears his name. He died in 1721 and the inscription on his grave reads:

Born in America, in Europe bred,
In Africa travell'd, and in Asia wed;
Where long he liv'd and thriv'd –
In London died:
Much good, some ill he did, so hope all's even,
And that his soul through mercy's gone to heav'n!
You that survive and read this tale, take care
For this most certain exit to prepare.
When blest in peace, the actions of the just
Smell sweet, and blossom in the silent dust.

Another name associated with Wrexham is that of the infamous Judge Jeffreys.

It has been suggested by one early biographer that the formation of

Jeffrey's twisted character may be attributed to a puritanical childhood, his parents being Dissenters. The first twelve years of his life were spent during what has become known as the Puritan ascendancy and, as one biographer rather quaintly points out, this was 'no doubt trying to vivacious children'. But the vivacious child grew into a cruel tyrant who was feared and hated during his lifetime!

Borrow was informed by a local that the only Welsh he was capable of speaking consisted of two words 'cwrw da', which translated means 'good ale'. Wrexham is justly famous for its lager which is brewed close to the town centre. Close by is the Racecourse, the ground of Wrexham Football Club. Loyalty to the Club is very strong in the area.

During the industrial revolution the area was of major importance in the production of iron and coal. A visit to the Bersham Ironworks and Heritage Centre sheds much light on the working class history of North-East Wales. But nowadays the new technology has taken over and companies like Sharp have a base on the edge of town, and the Japanese have not been slow to respond to the business opportunities which exist in Wrexham.

Chapter Two

LLANGOLLEN - VALLE CRUCIS - RUTHIN

Wales to Borrow was a

> 'land of old renown and of wonder, the land of Arthur and Merlin.'

He wished to know more about this defiant nation in the West in order to satisfy his enthusiastic curiosity about its history, literature and people. This was the motivation behind his visit in 1854.

Llangollen was a good central point for his excursions into other parts of the country and, from the outset, he had it in mind to write a book about his experiences. This was made clear by Mrs Borrow when she wrote to her mother-in-law soon after their arrival in Wales:

> 'George is fully occupied. He keeps a daily journal of all that goes on, so that he can make a most amusing book in a month...'

They arrived in Wales on 1st August and stayed until mid-November, but, contrary to what Mrs Borrow wrote, the book was not begun until much later. It must have demanded both time and effort, and was not published until 1862.

The Borrows, together with Mrs Borrow's daughter Henrietta – Borrow's step daughter – found lodgings at Dee Cottage in the town:

> '...it was called a cottage though it consisted of two storeys...Its front was towards a large orchard, which sloped down gently to the banks of the Dee; its back was towards the road leading from Wrexham, behind which was a high bank, on the top of which was a canal...'

During their period at the cottage the Borrows befriended a cat, which, it was said, had belonged to a former vicar of the parish. However when he departed he left the cat behind to fend for itself. The subsequent cleric owned dogs and they quickly drove the cat out. Borrow was led to believe that the majority of the population of Llangollen – some 3000 at that time – were dissenters and that many held unshakeable and quite irrational anti-Anglican feelings. Realising that the poor cat had lived with the former vicar they quickly dubbed it 'the church cat' and persecuted it whenever the opportunity arose. Borrow explained that the punishment which it experienced was

'...sorely on account of the opinions which it was supposed to have imbibed from its late master.'

He goes on to tell us:

'If the workmen of the flannel factory chanced to get a glimpse of it on the road from the windows of the building, they would sally forth in a body, and with sticks, stones or for want of other weapons, with clots of horse-dung would chase it...'

The commotion which the cat caused defies belief and it seems likely that Borrow was revealing his gullibility in relating the tale at all. His very strong Anglican feelings no doubt played a part here, but one cannot help feeling surprised that a man of his intellectual capabilities should have been duped in this way.

In retracing Borrow's footsteps there can be no more appropriate place to begin than at Dee Cottage, and on a pleasant October morning I knocked a little nervously at the back door. Our presence was heralded not by a cat but by a black Labrador. Gordon Pattinson, a retired college lecturer, and his wife are the present owners, and when I explained my interest in Borrow to Mrs Pattinson she invited us in. Her husband could not join us for coffee as he was laid low with flu, but as we sat in the pleasant 'parlour', where the Borrow's spent so many of their evenings, she told us that Borrovian enthusiasts and scholars have visited the cottage from as far afield as America and New Zealand, but curiously not from Wales. I asked her what she thought of the story of the 'church cat' and she agreed that it was too incredible to be given any credence.

After leaving Dee Cottage, my wife Pamela and I decided to ascend to Castell Dinas Brân. Beginning near Dinas Brân Comprehensive School a footpath takes the walker up a clearly signposted route. For the final phase, which is particularly steep, handrails curve around the conical hillside and hard-core has been provided underfoot.

According to Borrow the view from the top is 'very extensive', and he continues:

> '...The day on which I made my first ascent was very clear, but I do not think that I saw the Wyddfa.'

We also failed to see the highest Welsh mountain due to the Autumnal mists and so contented ourselves by gazing down at the Dee valley and Llangollen, which took on the perspective of a toy-town below us. The Dee, glittering in the afternoon sun, curved down the vale and I was reminded of what William Hazlitt in old age wrote in recalling a youthful visit:

> 'O sylvan Dee, in joy, in youth and gladness as thou then wert; and thou shalt always be to me the river of Paradise, where I will drink of the waters of life freely.'

It is easy to see why Dinas Brân became a part of Welsh iconography for poets and painters in the late eighteenth and early nineteenth centuries. It is spectacular by any standards, a picturesque landmark which compels one to climb to the summit.

The castle was probably built in the thirteenth century by order of Gruffydd ap Madog, but it would seem that there was an earlier fortification on the same site. It was captured by Dafydd ap Llewelyn in about 1282, but was taken later by English invaders, and eventually began to fall into ruin.

Such a romantic spot has to provide a role for a beautiful girl and Dinas Brân was no exception. Tradition has it that her name was Myfanwy and that she lived in the castle in the fourteenth century. The nineteenth century Welsh poet John Ceiriog Hughes wrote of her love for a bard named Hywel ab Einion.

Certain historical threads also link Owain Glyndŵr with Dinas Brân and in one of his major novels, 'Owain Glendower', that sadly neglected author John Cowper Powys brings together facets of this historical association.

It must be an irritant to many Welshmen, as it is to me, that in the title the much anglicised variant of Glyndŵr's name is used. One cannot imagine a writer of Powys' integrity accepting this lightly, but the decision was probably made by his publishers in order to attract as many English readers as possible.

Glyndŵr's name is inextricably linked with the whole of North East Wales and, at the time of writing, a district council administering part of the region is the Glyndŵr Council; an example of how we sometimes fall back on the history of Wales in order to shape coherent contemporary social patterns.

When he travelled through North Wales less than a hundred years ago A.G. Bradley related how he encountered old men living in the Dee Valley who would still talk of Glyndŵr as if he were still alive. The unrecorded past can be lost in a generation; how vastly rural Wales and its people have changed within the last hundred years.

Some months previously Pamela, had written a poem inspired by a visit to Dinas Brân:

> Massive mound reaching skywards
> Crowned with regal ruins of a fortress
> Crow castle, loftily enduring,
> Recalling primitive warfare.
> Ramparts from a previous time.
> Firm foundations built on rocks
> Survey the clefts and valleys
> Tumbled turrets rest on green turf,
> Where man can for a short time
> Scan distant horizons, breathe crisp air
> Rest pounding heart and gasping lungs
> Recover from the spiral climb.
> And from the precipitous landmark,
> Claim that today he reached the summit.

Back in the town we headed for a particularly large book store in Castle Street. In very extensive premises are thousands of second-hand books and you can browse through volume after volume, and if you have the time to spare you might save yourself the actual price of a book by reading it on the spot. The store had no Welsh interest section – a serious omission – and I searched in vain in the travel section for copies of Borrow's book, but none were available. I asked a young man in an inner office:

'Do you ever have copies of Borrow's "Wild Wales" in stock?'

His eyes glazed over and he responded with surly indifference:

'I dunno. We may have, but then we might not.'

I was tempted to ask him how he came to be selling books at all, but held my tongue and ambled out to join my wife on the street outside.

After my salutary experience I felt in need of a drink, and so we made for the nearest pub. It was quite crowded, for we were visiting the town during a white-water sporting event which was taking place on the Dee and canoeists and their followers seemed to have taken the town over.

As I drank my pint of lager I reflected on Borrow's comments on Llangollen ale. He was told by a local of the genuine malt and hop liquor brewed in a way only known to a few people in the town.

Borrow then proceeded to pen a quatrain:

'Llangollen's brown ale is with malt and hop rife;
    Tis good; but don't quaff it from evening till dawn;
For too much of that ale will incline you to strife;
    Too much of that ale causes knives to be drawn.'

Llangollen had a widespread reputation for the high quality and potency of its ale in the nineteenth century, as this anonymous doggerel illustrates:

While other poets loudly rant
About Llangollen's Vale,
Let me, with better taste, descant
Upon Llangollen Ale.

The daughters of the place are fair,
Its sons are strong and hale:
What makes them so? Llangollen air?
No, no! – Llangollen Ale.

And Nature only beautified
The landscape, to prevail
On travellers to turn aside
And quaff Llangollen Ale.

For though the scene might please at first
Its charms would quickly stale;
While he who tastes will ever thirst
To drink Llangollen Ale.

In short, each ruin, stream, or tree,
Within Llangollen's Vale,
Where'er I turn, whate'er I see,
Is redolent of Ale.

We spent that night at a hotel called the 'Sarah Ponsonby', named after the two illustrious ladies of Llangollen, the other being Eleanor Butler. These eccentric women eloped from their aristocratic homes in Ireland in an attempt to escape what they clearly regarded as the stifling conventions of their provincial background.

With their maid, Mary, they settled at Plas Newydd, a highly timbered house in Llangollen in 1780. Borrow reminds us that they were famous throughout Europe, which is astonishing when you consider that there was no media in those days, and only limited newspaper coverage of British news. Many luminaries visited them including Wellington, Burke, Shelley, Wordsworth, Byron and Sir Walter Scott. Wordsworth displeased them by making a reference to their home as 'a low roof'd cot' in one of his poems. Borrow, however, payed posthumous homage when he was at Plas Newydd, for both the Ladies had by that time been dead for well over two decades. But he was able to speak to a local who knew a great deal about them and could clearly recall their arrival in the town. I assume that had the Ladies been alive in 1854 Borrow may well have paid them a visit and it is tempting to imagine what the encounter would have been like.

Today Plas Newydd is featured in Wales Tourist Board brochures and attracts many different kinds of visitors, from studious Americans from state universities to day-trippers from Birmingham and Manchester.

The building seems to me to be too obviously an effort on the part of the designer, or architect, to make it conform to eighteenth century expectations of the picturesque. Looking at the exterior is almost like viewing the large set for a highly ambitious stage play.

* * *

The Llangollen canal is a further much publicised tourist attraction, and as we strolled at a leisurely pace along the towpath in the direction of Trevor we were overtaken by motor-powered barges and a quietly moving horse drawn pleasure barge. Surely travelling by water on the elaborate canal system must, apart from walking, be the most pleasurable way of getting around, but I wonder whether I could master all those locks?

The canals developed during the ever-increasing industrialisation which took place in the second half of the early eighteenth century, and the one at Llangollen facilitated the transportation of large quantities of slate. Borrow spoke to one man who had travelled as far afield as Paddington, and on such a journey, which normally took three weeks, he would be accompanied by his wife and children.

We eventually arrived at that monument to the supreme enterprise of Thomas Telford, Froncysyllte Aqueduct, which takes both barge passengers and pedestrians one hundred and twenty six feet over the Dee Valley to the Chirk side.

Borrow was told by a local guide:

'...it's the finest bridge in the world, and no wonder, if what the common people say be true, namely that every stone cost a golden sovereign.'

As they walked over to the far side Borrow admitted that he found the height 'awful'. He adds:

'I too felt somewhat dizzy as I looked over the parapet into the glen.'

I could not express my own feelings more aptly as I gazed down at the Dee far below; a bird's eye view indeed!

* * *

On a walk to Ruthin, up the area now commonly known as the 'Horseshoe Pass', Borrow was reminded of certain similar passes in Spain. He stopped to look at Valle Crucis Abbey, which impressed him:

'The vale or glen in which the abbey stands takes its name from a certain ancient pillar or cross called the pillar of Eliseg, and which is believed to have been raised over the body of an ancient British chieftain of that name, who perished in battle against the Saxons, about the middle of the tenth century.'

But it is not only a chieftain who is reputed to be buried in that small area, for it is believed that the great fourteenth century poet Iolo Goch was laid to rest at the Abbey. He hailed from the Vale of Clwyd and became a very close friend of Owain Glyndŵr, with whom he lived at Sycharth. Borrow was very aware of Iolo Goch's importance, for he wrote:

'He composed pieces of great excellence on various subjects; but the most remarkable of his compositions are decidedly certain ones connected with Glyndŵr.'

But more on this in a future chapter.

Standing close to that part of the building where the monks had lived was a farmhouse, from which an old countrywoman emerged and invited Borrow in. When he addressed her in Welsh she was pleased:

'She said that Welsh people at the present day were so full of fine airs that they were above speaking the old language.'

When asked if she had heard of Iolo Goch she said she had not, but added that she could show him a portrait of a greater poet. She then produced a print in a frame:

'There,' said she, 'is a portrait of Twm o'r Nant, generally called the Welsh Shakespeare.'

It was not, therefore, Borrow who made this exalted comparison, as is sometimes assumed, but the Welsh people.

As Borrow was departing the old woman begged him to taste the water at a nearby holy well.

'What holy well is that?' said I.
'A well,' said she, 'by the road's side which in the time of the popes were said to perform wonderful cures.'

The pillar of Eliseg stands on a mound within a couple of hundred yards of the abbey.

'The view from the column is very beautiful' Borrow reflected.

It would be so today but for the deplorable presence of a caravan site within very close proximity to the abbey. As I gazed at this incongruous scene in the mellow Autumn sunshine my thoughts were not as elevated as Borrow's, and I reflected on the result of a totally stupid decision of some planning committee or other.

* * *

The predominant impression of Llangollen which Borrow conveys is of an unequivocably Welsh community. But today, of course, it is highly anglicised, indeed cosmopolitan. Apart from being the annual venue of the International Musical Eisteddfod, when the entire world seems to converge on this small town to sing and dance for a week, it also has the ECTARC centre; the European Centre for Traditional and Regional Cultures.

During our weekend in the town we did not hear any Welsh spoken at all, whereas Borrow had encountered certain individuals who raised interesting, perspectives on the entire subject of what it means to be Welsh.

A blacksmith named Joseph Hughes took great pride in being 'a real Welshman'. He had developed a strong antipathy towards the English because they were in the habit of ridiculing his Welshness:

'I told him that all Englishmen were not fools. 'But the greater part are' said he...'There seems to be something of the old Celtic hatred to the Saxon in this old fellow' said I to myself as I walked away.'

But even today there is, of course, much muddled thinking about Wales on the part of the English, and this has been partly the result of stereotyping.

A classic example occurred in the late nineteen thirties when the Holywood film director John Ford decided to transfer Richard Llewelyn's best-selling novel "How Green Was My Valley" to the cinema screen. Llewelyn's novel has much to commend it, but the film proved to be a travesty of the book. In one dreadful scene blackened miners walk briskly and jauntily home from a day of unremitting toil singing a Welsh hymn joyously.

But, more recently, false images of Welshness have come from within Wales. The comedian Max Boyce, with his sometimes exaggerated South Wales accent, his leek and his football scarf, conveys to audiences outside Wales an image which some may be gullible enough to accept as a representation of a 'typical' Welshman. In truth, of course, there is no such thing as a 'typical Welshman' anymore than there is a 'typical Englishman' or a 'typical Scotsman'. Each nation consists of a population of individuals not cloned models.

Borrow was made aware of the divide between two nations on a number of occasions. One man whom he paused to chat to claimed that:

'...there was a time when it was customary for the English to cut off the ears of every Welshman who was found to the east of Offa's Dyke, and for the Welsh to hang every Englishman whom they found to the west of it.'

Well, things have changed quite a lot since then, and yet despite these changes there are still seemingly irreconcilable differences. Some years ago the poet Harri Webb summed these up from a Welsh perspective when he said that he wished that Wales had an eastern coastline. I don't think he was talking literally, but it is not hard to see what may have prompted such a statement.

Central government attitudes to Wales have been resented by many Welshmen and their indifference to the wish of the Welsh people for an assembly which would ensure political autonomy is a burning issue. The appointments, over a period of decades, of Tory secretaries of state is much resented by many in Wales. What, it is asked, do these privileged members of parliament for affluent English constituencies know of the problems and needs of Wales?

In the window of a Llangollen bookshop I spotted a glossy paperback biography of Prince Charles and this set my thoughts running yet again along radical lines.

* * *

'About three miles to the north is a range of lofty mountains, dividing the shire of Denbigh from that of Flint, among which, lifting its head above the rest is the mighty Moel Famau, the mother heap, which I had seen from Chester.'

There was this curious tendency among literary tourists to regard as mountains what we would today describe as only high hills. By no stretch of the imagination is Moel Famau a mountain and to describe everyone who walks to the summit – as I have a number of times – as a mountaineer would be ridiculous.

Borrow has little to add about the Clwydian hills and the valley below, which is perhaps, a little surprising. He did, however, spend a little time at Ruthin, and devotes a page or so to the town. He reveals a somewhat ambivalent attitude when he writes:

'Ruthin is a dull town, but it possessed plenty of interest for me...'

He was clearly moved by the fact that he found himself in a town which had figured so prominently during the tempestuous Glyndŵr rebellion.

He was

'...where the great struggle commenced which for fourteen years convulsed Wales, and for some time shook England to its centre.'

The other major protagonist in this long conflict was Reginald de Grey, who was granted the lordship of Ruthin in 1282. On a fair day in 1400 Glyndŵr brought all his armed fury down on the town, but failed to capture the castle.

Indeed, in general terms, Glyndŵr's military actions took a heavy toll on both property and human life in North East Wales and the borders, and nowadays historians tend to agree that as a rebel and campaign strategist he made many mistakes. But, as Sir John Lloyd wrote

'...his name has been one of power in Wales: attempts to reduce him to the stature of a robber thief and lawless brigand have been ineffectual to quench the national devotion to his memory...He may with propriety be called the father of Welsh nationalism.'

Standing in the town centre my predominant impression was of the neatness and compactness of Ruthin when compared to the neighbouring town of Denbigh. St Peter's Square is one of the finest in Wales and creates an impression of affluence. Walk down between the fine church and the almshouses and you could be in a small corner of Anthony Trollope's Barchester; it is an altogether delightful spot, and I like the way in which, no matter where one may be in Ruthin, one is aware of being little more than a stone's-throw – or so it seems – from the pastoral loveliness of the Clwydians.

In the evening we attended a concert in the town hall organised by the local music society. There was a large audience and the instrumentalist who had been engaged was the brilliant triple harpist Robin Huw Bowen, who has established a virtual one-man crusade in an attempt to promote the instrument. He is the only professional harpist specialising in this instrument alone and as he played 'Clychau Aberdyfi', 'Dawns y Tylwyth Teg', 'Llwyn Onn', and many other traditional airs, I could not help reflecting on how Borrow would have relished the occasion.

During the interval I fell into conversation with a sharp-featured middle aged man, who, I gathered, was an official of the music society.

'I've always thought that if I'm lucky enough to get to heaven one day then I'll be quite happy if there is music like this being played there' he said, with a twinkle in his eye.

'You should be writing Robin's publicity material,' I joked. 'He'll never find a higher recommendation than that.'

We both laughed as we returned to our seats to enjoy more of the wonderful melodies of Wales.

In a musical context Ruthin has a little known claim to fame in Welsh musical life, for although 'Hen Wlad fy Nhadau' was composed in South Wales it took the expertise of a Ruthinian to print the first copies. The printing works of Isaac Clark stood at the rear of the building now occupied by a cafe and gift shop in Well Street. Unfortunately in 1898 Clark ran into financial difficulties and he was forced to give up his press. He was also responsible for the printing of the Bible and produced a musical journal, but his contribution to Welsh culture has, sadly, been largely overlooked by historians.

* * *

On the journey back to Llangollen Borrow described visiting a Baptist chapel but failed to tell us where this is situated. In actual fact this neat, small former place of worship is situated approximately a mile from the village of Llanfair Dyffryn Clwyd, on the right hand side of the road which leads to Graigfechan.

Soon afterwards he found himself in pleasant grounds and on asking a passer-by the name of the place was informed that it was called Oaklands because of the large number of fine oaks in the area. He wondered why a Saxon name had been given to a place in Wales and learned that the trees were planted by an English family.

Today the name Oaklands will no longer be found on the map, for the house and its grounds – now a farm – have, at last, assumed a Welsh name.

Chapter Three

DYFFRYN CEIRIOG

Accompanied by the Llangollen weaver, John Jones, Borrow was taken over the hills to Pontymeibion which Jones supposed was the birthplace of the great seventeenth century poet Huw Morys. However it has not proved possible to definitely ascertain the whereabouts of his birthplace, for the Morys family, being fairly affluent, owned land and property both at Hafodgynfor in the parish of Llangollen and in the Ceiriog valley. According to both the 'Dictionary of Welsh Biography' and 'The Oxford Companion to the Literature of Wales' Morys was born at Hafodgynfor, the family moving to Pontymeibion in 1647.

Other sources state that he was born at Pontymeibion, but I am more inclined to regard the two publications mentioned as being more authoritative.

He disliked what he regarded as the uncongenial life of a farmer and was drawn increasingly into the writing of poetry when quite young. When the Civil War erupted in 1642 Huw sided with the Royalist cause, but not as a combatant but rather as a literary propagandist. He wrote in eloquent terms expressing his loyalty to Charles I while at the same time composing bitter satire against the Roundheads. But he did not descend to slander, and his tact in this respect meant that he was able to avoid persecution.

He regarded as highly dangerous the ideas of such Puritan contemporaries as Walter Cradock and Morgan Llwyd. He was held in extremely high regard by the people of Denbighshire and was warden of Llansilin Church. The high opinion of fellow worshippers was recalled by Borrow:

'It was the custom in those days in North Wales for the congregation to leave the church in a row with the clergyman at their head, but so great was the estimation in which old Huw was held, for the purity of his life and poetical gift, that the clergyman of the parish abandoning his claim to precedence, always insisted on the good and inspired old man's leading the file, himself following immediately in the rear.'

Erw Gerrig, which is next door to Pontymeibion, was evidently also owned by the Morys family, for very close to this former farm the stone bardic chair was erected in which he would, no doubt, compose verses. When Borrow was searching for the chair he was taken by a local girl into something of a wilderness with 'a maze of tangled shrubs...thorns, tall nettles and small trees'. They at last found

'...a mouldering stone slab forming the seat, and a large slate stone, the back, on which were cut the letters –
H.M.B.
signifying Huw Morys Bard.'

Borrow sat on the chair and repeated verses by the poet, who became known as 'the Nightingale of Ceiriog', while Jones and the girl

'...listened patiently and approvingly though the rain was pouring down upon them.'

He continues:

'...enthusiasm is never scoffed at by the noble, simple minded, genuine Welsh whatever treatment it may receive from the coarse-headed Saxon.'

The chair may still be seen today, although it has within recent years been moved slightly from its original location. It has assumed the status of a nationally important feature in literary terms within North Wales.

We had no difficulty in finding it thanks to the very helpful present owner of Erw Gerrig, Anne Kynaston. As I stood looking at it, it began to rain, and I reflected that, perhaps, I was seeing it more or less as Borrow did on that wet day in 1854.

As we sat in Mrs Kynaston's kitchen afterwards she revealed her passionate interest in the poet, and produced nineteenth century editions of his work, photocopies of items about him, and letters from academics and researchers. I asked her what had brought her to this important literary shrine and she proceeded to relate a remarkable story.

When she took on this farm house and its eighty eight acres there was much work to be done.

'You see the farm house here and the buildings were more or less derelict,' she told us. 'My two sons were away at university and I was really on my own. I think some of my neighbours must have wondered whether I would make it as a farmer through my first winter. You see there wasn't actually a roof on the house and I was forced to live under tarpaulin. There were no mod-cons at all, no water, no electricity, no sanitation.'

If this seems remarkable, it is even more remarkable to learn how Mrs Kynaston spent her first Christmas at the farm.

'I was really living in a hovel at that time, I suppose,' she reflected. 'My warmth came from a fire in a bucket and with my back against a wall I sat staring at a Christmas tree. I couldn't help wondering what the boys would say when they came home.'

Her sons were only too willing to work hard in an effort to rebuild the house. Other students also came along and worked on the land. Having put in an enormous amount of work she eventually decided to put the farm buildings and the land and stock up for sale, but remained in the house.

'What did you do then?' I asked.

'Well I decided to take a catering course, and at the end of it I was awarded a City and Guild certificate. I wanted to do what a lot of people were doing then, to go into the farmhouse holiday business.'

She offers self-catering accommodation and bed and breakfast in highly comfortable surroundings.

Anne Kynaston is a remarkable person, and it came as no surprise to learn that some years ago BBC radio had devoted an entire programme to her.

Later Borrow and Jones visited a 'small tavern' at Pandy, a hamlet close to Glyn Ceiriog.

Here they encountered an inebriated young man who was a stone mason. He

'...talked very incoherently about the war [the Crimean War] saying that he hoped it would soon terminate for if it continued he was afraid he might stand a chance of being shot, as he was a private in the Denbighshire Militia.'

Borrow then proceeded to goad him by pompously telling him that it was

'...the duty of every gentleman in the militia to be willing at all times to lay down his life in the service of the Queen.'

But when the militiaman learned that Borrow had been to see the chair of Huw Morys his interest was immediately aroused. In a highly slurred manner he proceeded to recite some melancholy lines by the poet:

'A scene in a public house, yes! but in a Welsh public-house. Only think of a Norfolk toper repeating the death-bed verses of a poet: surely there is a considerable difference between the Celt and the Saxon.'

Think of that unique national institution the National Eisteddfod. The very thought of a very large audience, from a variety of social backgrounds, packing a pavilion to hear the proclamation of the identity of a prize-winning poet, before a blaze of media publicity, in, say Bath or Chichester defies the imagination. It could only happen in Wales.

A poet who appears to have been rather critical of the Eisteddfod, and who is not mentioned by Borrow, is John Ceiriog Hughes. This major nineteenth century lyric poet, who wrote work which has been extremely highly rated, was an exile from Wales for a time. When he returned he became an employee of the Cambrian Railway Company in the capacity of stationmaster and later, following promotion, in a more senior position. This was a creatively fruitful period of his life, and he frequented local literary circles and entered into lively gossip with fellow poets.

The words of a number of his poems have been set to music and have remained popular, including 'Nant y Mynydd' and 'Dafydd y Garreg Wen'. He also wrote the words of that sycophantic song 'God Bless the Prince of Wales'.

On the main street of Glyn Ceiriog you will find the Institute, or village hall. This was built with donations from throughout Wales and the plaque outside reminds us that it was

'...the practical outcome of the Welsh spiritual revival of 1904-5 commonly associated with the name of Evan Roberts. It was founded in 1911...'

Here can be seen stained glass windows which perpetuate the memory of Hughes, Huw Morys and Borrow himself.

Dyffryn Ceiriog, which cuts like a cleft into the Berwyn hills, is one of the loveliest valleys in Wales, and Glyn Ceiriog is a delightful village. Although it is a mere three miles or so from the English border it has, to a remarkable extent, retained its Welshness. In Borrow's time it was an industrial community with three large quarries and four woollen mills. Nowadays, like other areas of rural Wales, it is heavily dependent on tourism.

Chapter Four

DYFFRYN EDEYRNION AND CORWEN

'I was now about to leave Llangollen for a short time, and to set out on an expedition to Bangor, Snowdon, and one or two places in Anglesey.'

Borrow set out in evident good spirits on a Sunday morning, and he chose this day of the week deliberately as he was

'...anxious to observe the general demeanour of the people on the Sabbath.'

He arranged for his wife and Henrietta to meet him in Bangor, to which they would travel by train, and, after seeing something of north west Wales they were to return in comfort to Dee Cottage, leaving our veteran walker to explore parts of Caernarfonshire and Ynys Môn.

Quickening his pace on a fine Autumn morning Borrow eventually left Llangollen behind him, and after an hour or so of energetic walking arrived at Dyffryn Edeyrnion. He soon found himself on a bridge fording the Dee, this being situated very close to the village of Carrog. On the bridge he fell into conversation with a man who was on his way home from a chapel service. Borrow, being the one-man inquisition that he was, did not waste any time before he interrogated the stranger about his religious persuasion. The man told him that he was a Calvinistic Methodist.

'Have you been to chapel, sir?' he asks Borrow.
'I do not go to chapel; I belong to the church.'
'Have you been to church, sir?'
'I have not – I said my prayers at home and then walked out.'
'It is not right to walk out on the Sabbath day except to go to church or chapel.'

Borrow, true to form, prolonged the argument, but the stranger became even more entrenched in the dogma of his faith:

> '...in Wales when we see a person walking idly about on the Sabbath day we are in the habit of saying "Sabbath breaker, where are you going?" '

How very strange Borrow's account of this conversation seems to us in our secular society. They may even have appeared a little daunting to certain readers of 'Wild Wales' when it was first published.

Walking further along the valley Borrow observed a pronounced mound, on which trees were growing. He was told by another local man that this was Owain Glyndŵr's mount.

> 'This is the hill of Owain Glyndŵr, sir, where he was in the habit of standing to look out for his enemies coming from Chester.'

The local was of the opinion that it was a man-made structure but that it was probably erected before Glyndŵr's time by ancient people who may have buried their leader on this spot.

> 'Heaps like this have frequently been opened and found to contain pots with ashes and bones'

comments Borrow.

As I made my way over a field to the mount I instinctively felt that someone was walking behind me. When I turned my head I saw a man who, from his dress, I immediately assumed was a farmer. He was leanly built, about sixty and had a collie with him.

'I'm just going to have a look at Glyndŵr's mount' I explained, in order to allay any fears he might have about me being a cattle rustler.

'That's alright,' he said without smiling, 'as long as you shut the gate after you when you leave. Where are you from?'

When I told him that my home was at Denbigh he smiled and asked whether I had stopped taking the tablets yet. This was an old joke which I had heard many times before and an allusion to the fact that the mental hospital for North Wales was, until recently, situated at Denbigh.

I responded with a tired, forced laugh.

'So you're interested in old Glyndŵr are you?' he asked warming to me suddenly. 'There are so many tales about him that is a job to know what's true and what isn't,' he continued, 'My father told me many a tale about him when I was a lad and he always said that he would rise from the grave again when Wales was in her hour of greatest need.'

'Well in that case,' I responded, 'it wouldn't be a bad idea for him to come back now to make sure Wales gets devolution.'

'Oh aye, I'm all for home rule too. And I'll tell you something else.' He paused and looked at me intently. 'If Owain did come back he could do a bloody sight worse than sort out the problems of us poor farmers. But old Glyndŵr was a great man there's no doubt about that.'

We parted from each other, he to look at his stock and I to look carefully at the mound. The farmer had referred to 'old Glyndŵr' and I reflected that he could have been talking about an uncle in the next valley or perhaps a favourite drinking companion in the local pub. Underneath the farmer's scepticism there appeared to be an underlying affection for the enigmatic leader. Glyndŵr can be all things to all Welshmen.

* * *

Borrow has little to tell us about Corwen and appears to have spent his time there sampling the ale at the principal inn, now the Owain Glyndŵr Hotel. A fairly large number of public houses – the Crown, the Harp and the Royal Oak among them – offered accommodation and refreshment to nineteenth century travellers, at a time when a busy and important stagecoach route ran through the town. Today, of course, this is the A5, along which motor vehicles thunder at speeds which would have been inconceivable to the Victorians.

I was struck by the fascinating juxtaposition of various business premises and other buildings. Cheek by jowl with Valentine's Tandoori Indian Restaurant was an ugly Wesleyan chapel, circa 1879, while a little way along was a cafe offering an exotic bonus to customers, for it was also advertising the sale of butterflies. Then there was a pub and an extremely austere church house. One of the smaller businesses was hiring out fancy dress costumes – are there many fancy dress parties in Corwen?

A small building on the edge of one of the town car parks is marked 'Mortuary'. I had visions of someone turning up at a fancy dress party full of life and leaving on a mortuary trolley!

In the town centre stands a bronze statue of Owain Glyndŵr, which was commissioned by the community council at a cost of £6.,000 and erected in 1995. Some people were fiercely critical of it, claiming that it was a poor representation of the leader. It soon came under the threat of vandalism, and, in fact, when I was in the process of researching this book had been stored for safekeeping in an animal feed warehouse on the edge of the town. After many inquiries I was able to track it down there in order to take a photograph. But in September 1996 it was reinstated as a public memorial, but this time on a higher plinth.

I can understand why this so-called work of art has aroused such strong feelings, for it is far from flattering to its subject and gives him the general appearance of an arthritic angler. I don't imagine it would have been approved of by the great novelist John Cowper Powys, the author of a magnificent, and very long, work of prose fiction based on the events of Glyndŵr's life. Powys, one of a remarkable literary family, came to live in Corwen in 1934, and remained here, living in an ordinary terraced house, for over twenty years, after which he moved to Blaenau Ffestiniog.

In the nineteen seventies Corwen had another well known resident for a period of about a year. This was Frank Serpico, who faced the possibility of death each day in his fight against corruption in the New York Police Department. He was a shattered man when he arrived at Corwen, but during his stay he regained much of his former physical and mental strength. His fame was such that his dangerous life became the subject of a long-running television series and also a Hollywood feature film.

We visited the church, which is on a sixth century site. Folklore has it that as the builders endeavoured to construct the original building a supernatural force would destroy their labour overnight. It is not clear how they got around this problem.

In the churchyard are a number of interesting graves and the inscription on that of Owen Owen caught my eye. He was an engine driver who had died at the age of twenty-nine:

'His life is over,
Death has put on the brake,
His soul has been signalled
Its long journey to make.

When death sounds his whistle
The steam of life fails
And his mortal clay shunted
Till the Last Judgement calls.'

There is a stone built into the church wall which bears a cross.

The eminent antiquary the Rev. Elias Owen in his book 'The Old

Stone Crosses of the Vale of Clwyd', published in 1886, writes of it:

> 'Local tradition speaks of this cross as being the impression of Owain
> Glyndŵr's dagger. It says that Glyndŵr hurled the dagger from the
> summit of the conical hill, which stands on the south side of the
> church and overlooks the town, with such force that it made a deep
> indentation in the stone it came in contact with.'

This is a further gem from the folklore of the area, one of the tales which
have both delighted and amused generations of local people. North Wales
generally is a rich depository of such tales.

* * *

On the evening following our visit to Edeyrnion I settled down to read
again T.E. Ellis' 'Speeches and Addresses', published in 1912, and came
upon these impressive reflections:

> 'It was not from a borough or a garrison town but from one of the
> glens of the Dee that Owain Glyndŵr rose to wage his fifteen years'
> memorable struggle for Wales. Huw Morys, Pont y Meibion, and
> Morgan Llwyd o Wynedd, the two Welsh voices of the seventeenth
> century, were country folk...From cottages nestling under the Berwyns
> have sprung typical men like Ceiriog, Ieuan Gwynedd and Owain
> Edwards. And there is no reason to suppose that the country districts
> will cease to form the nursery ground of men of thought, initiative
> and influence.'

T.E. Ellis himself deserves to be added to this array of names, for he was
what is now, in a world of political liars and cheats, a rare combination.
He was a politician of great integrity and also a highly cultured man, who
cared deeply about the future of Wales.

Chapter Five

CERRIGYDRUDION TO BANGOR

Nowadays some of Borrow's inquisitive questions to people whom he encountered would probably earn him at best an angry rebuff and at worst a black eye. But he creates the impression that no unpleasantness resulted from his demanding probing. When he stayed at the Lion Inn at Cerrigydrudion he met an itinerant Italian who was travelling around trying to sell weather glasses:

> I asked him if he was married.
> 'No, signore, but my brother in Liverpool is.'
> 'To an Italian?'
> 'No, signore, to a Welsh girl.'
> 'And I suppose,' said I, 'you will follow his example by marrying one; perhaps that good looking girl, the landlady's daughter, we were seated with last night?'

Such probing reveals a further unacceptable facet to Borrow's personality, but then, of course, one has to take into account that he may have exaggerated situations in order to instill his writing with greater interest.

In the following chapter he recalls a meeting with 'a fellow with red hair and very red features' with a game leg. He is a Dublin Catholic and, in view of Borrow's anti papist prejudices, escapes quite lightly.

Eventually Borrow arrives at

> ...a small village at the entrance of which was a waterwheel – near the village was a gentleman's seat almost surrounded by groves'.

This is Pentrefoelas, a good example of an estate village. At about the time that Borrow was there it was an extremely flourishing community, as the following anonymous piece of poetry makes clear:

In 'Pentref y Foelas', in order, we see
Vocations, the number of forty less three;
They exist all together, all pleasant, serene,
Although of the dwellings there are but seventeen;
Publican, shopkeeper, for stranger and kith,
A draper, a farmer, a saddler and smith,
A labourer, gravedigger, carpenter of skill,
A baker; a barber and the 'man of the mill'.
A bookbinder, preacher and gardener are seen,
Turner, nailer and cobbler and postmaster keen,
A vet and a tanner, a cooper at hand,
A priest and the doctor – the best in the land,
An embroidress, a bakeress, one who tends to the hues,
Paperhangers and painter, hands turned to all use;
Watchmaker, bellringer, ostler for the mount,
Schoolmaster and butcher all add to the count;
To maintain rule and order as well as can be
There are also a constable and a local J.P.,
And in order to finish the portrait withal.
A literary society for the poet, and all.

The Wynne family at Voelas Hall made donations to assist the provision of an adequate education for village children, as well as providing employment. Up to about fifty years ago Pentrefoelas was a thriving community, but during the following two or three decades villagers were increasingly forced to move to other areas in their search for work. But now the village has been granted a new lease of life due to the tremendous emphasis on the importance of tourism in the Welsh economy within the last decade. Due to the sponsorship of various organisations the old greystone buildings have now been restored. Workplaces have been opened up once more by craftpeople and the watermill again produces stoneground flour. A heritage trail takes visitors to all these buildings and stone plaques convey historical information.

Pentrefoelas may be regarded as a part of the Hiraethog region, which once stimulated a rich peasant tradition of poetry and song. This concept of the men of the bare hillside making art out of what they are, and where they are, is one which has great appeal for me.

Hiraethog is a region, but there appears to be some difficulty in defining where its boundaries lie. This will explain my hint about a cautious approach in deciding whether certain villages are in Hiraethog or not. There is no doubt in my mind that Gwytherin and Llansannan are well within the boundaries, and Pentrefoelas no doubt qualifies as well, but what about villages on the Denbigh side of that great stretch of moorland dividing it from Pentrefoelas and the A5, such as Bylchau, Nantglyn and Groes?

Perhaps one day some enterprising sociologist may write a paper on this subject; it would make interesting reading.

* * *

Betws-y-Coed exemplifies the high profile of tourism in Wales, for if you walk through the village on any day during the summer months you will encounter a bustling community.

In Borrow's time Betws attracted the fashionable gentry, including fishing enthusiasts, and water-colour painters. He observed

'...neat dwellings for the accommodation of visitors, with cool apartments on the ground-floor with large windows, looking towards the precipitous side of the mighty hill'.

Inside were

'tables and books and young men, probably English collegians, seated at study'.

Attempts are constantly being made by the media to create a sense of nostalgia, often for a period which we did not know, and, having read accounts of Victorian and Edwardian Betws I would like to travel back to those bygone decades. I could then meet the painter David Cox and watch him painting some of his finest work, or, a little more recently, meet Sir Edward Elgar, who stayed in the area for several weeks while he was composing 'The Dream of Gerontius'.

Borrow did what all visitors to Betws-y-coed do, and went to see the Swallow Falls, that wonderful cataract of seething white water, which one descends to down steps from the road in order to view it to full advantage. His description is characteristically vivid:

'First there are a number of little foaming torrents, bursting through rocks about twenty yards from the promontory on which I stood. Then come two beautiful rolls of white water, dashing into a pool a

44

little way above the promontory; then there is a swirl of water round its corner into a pool below on its right, black as death and seemingly of great depth; then a rush through a very narrow outlet into another pool, from which the water clamours away down the glen.'

There is evidence from tourist accounts that in the mid-nineteenth century, as today, people were being asked for money for the privilege of seeing the Falls. Exploiting the natural assets of Wales in this way is something which I am opposed to. By all means charge natives and visitors admission fees to ancient monument sites, such as castles, for these precious buildings have to be maintained at considerable expense. But to capitalise on natural features of the Welsh countryside, like the Swallow Falls, smacks of greed on somebody's part.

Borrow found the area between Betws and Capel Curig to be

'...a region of fairy beauty and wild grandeur'.

While enjoying the peace of his surroundings he met a local man who was so surprised that Borrow, an Englishman, was able to speak in Welsh that he exclaimed:

'It will be a thing to talk of for the rest of my life'.

Such a reaction would never occur today. Within the last two decades, or longer, there has been in influx of English settlers in all areas of rural Wales. I am not here thinking so much of the hippies who moved into communes in the hinterlands in the seventies, but rather of professional middle class families who now either run businesses in the country, or are at least involved in some form of work which benefits the Welsh economy. Many of these people have made a determined attempt to learn the Welsh language, and they are delighted that their children are being educated within the medium of Welsh. Paradoxically many Welsh-born people do not speak the language and are not actively making any attempt to do so. Yet many of them would claim that they are not fully accepted as Welsh due to their linguistic inability and, as they feel completely Welsh, and perhaps vote for Plaid Cymru (as I do), they are forced to the conclusion that this schism is unfortunate.

On reaching Capel Curig Borrow decided to take rest and refreshment for he had

'...walked now twenty miles on a broiling day'.

At a hotel he

'...dined in a grand saloon amidst a great deal of fashionable company'.

When we made a stop at the village we visited the Pinnacle Cafe for tea and scones. Half of the other tables were occupied by people who, it was fairly obvious, were tourists.

I fell into conversation with a tall, darkly complexioned middle-aged man at the next table. He was a college lecturer who had travelled from Southern Brittany to holiday in Wales for the first time, an experience which he was evidently enjoying very much. As I had been in Brittany as a member of a cultural group a few months previously this allowed me to exchange opinions with him concerning the widely recognised affinities between the two countries.

'Of course you in Wales have been treated like colonials, as we have,' he said, and I was quick to confirm this in an animated way. 'Why,' he went on, 'did your nation reject devolution in 1979?'

'Do you know,' I replied sadly, 'that is something which I think about a lot. It haunts me sometimes. It is incomprehensible and I will never begin to understand why.'

'You lost a golden opportunity there' was his response.

* * *

Borrow continued his journey to Bangor, passing through Bethesda – 'a scriptural name' he comments – and on arriving at the end of this lap of his journey he tells us that

'...Bangor was once a place of Druidical worship, of which fact, even without the testimony of history and tradition the name which signifies "upper circle" would be sufficient evidence. On the decay of Druidism a town sprang up on the site...'

He refers to two poets who have associations with the city, Taliesin and Edmwnd Prys, both of whom

'...conferred a kind of lustre on Bangor by residing in it'.

Taliesin he describes as of 'the end of the fifth century', although it seems that Borrow was a century out here, for it is now generally agreed that he lived in the sixth century.

Prys, on the other hand, was a sixteenth century figure, who was born at Llanrwst. His wealth of scholarship combined with his poetic skill, made him a formidable figure. He pursued an illustrious ecclesiastical career and, like many clerics of that period, became fairly wealthy and owned land at Maentwrog and other areas of Snowdonia.

Possibly, in one respect, Borrow may have felt a sense of affinity with Prys through their linguistic abilities: both had mastered a number of languages. In a cywydd Prys reveals this side of his learning:

'I've read the masterpieces great
Of languages no less than eight,
But ne'er have found a woof of song
So strict as that of Cambria's tongue.'

Two literary figures of our own century who have become inextricably associated with Bangor are Kate Roberts and R.S. Thomas. Both were partly educated at the university college.

Kate Roberts is now widely accepted as the foremost novelist and short story writer in Welsh in the twentieth century. She was born at Rhosgadfan, a village in the Caernarfonshire hills, into a working class family, and the early material struggle which she experienced is clearly reflected in her writing. In the mid-nineteen thirties she bought Gwasg Gee at Denbigh, the oldest publishing company in Wales. Her husband died in 1946 and she lived on for a further four decades, and during the last twenty years of her life I got to know her personally. It is only really since her death that a determined effort has been made to give her the recognition she so clearly deserves outside Wales. One person who was instrumental in this process was an American professor, Joseph Clancy and his large volume of translations of Kate Roberts' work entitled 'The World of Kate Roberts', was published by an American press.

R.S. Thomas is one of the finest Welsh language poets writing in English. In my opinion, and that of certain critics and fellow-poets, he stands among the very greatest of modern poets, comparable in stature to Yeats and Eliot. In old age he now lives on Ynys Môn where he continues to write and also to indulge his other great passion, birdwatching.

If we think of Bangor's role as an educational centre we may well tend to think of it only in terms of the university. But in College Road is the regional office of the North Wales branch of the Workers Educational

Association, the WEA. The director is an old friend of mine, Rufus Adams, whose dedication to the Association over the years has been unstinting.

As we sat in his office we reflected on the changing image of the WEA during the last sixty years. In the thirties and forties the courses which were organised attracted, as intended, a predominantly working-class following. These adult students were anxious to enhance their knowledge, for these were people who had failed to reach their true potential while at school.

So the WEA, and the residential college Coleg Harlech, gave them the opportunity of a second chance, enabling them to reach their level of achievement academically. I write from personal experience here for I attended WEA courses in my late teens, having been the product of an uncaring secondary modern school. This led directly to my becoming a full-time student at Coleg Harlech for two years. One of the young tutors at the college at that time – 1959, – was Rufus Adams, whose commitment to adult education over the years is something for which many can now be thankful.

Borrow, unlike myself, did not encounter anyone in Bangor with anything of particular interest to tell him. He relates a conversation with an itinerant Irish bookseller but there is no real point to it; the bookseller addresses Borrow as 'your hanner', a reverential term which tends to irritate the egalitarian reader.

Later he sees

'...a number of wild-looking people, male and female...All the females had common tin articles in their hands which they offered for sale with violent gestures to the people in the streets, as they walked along, occasionally darting into shops, from which however, they were almost invariably ejected by the startled proprietors, with looks of disgust and almost horror'.

A bypasser to whom Borrow speaks considers this band of Irish tinkers "a disgrace to their country".

'I did not exactly think so' writes Borrow. 'I thought that in many respects they were fine specimens of humanity.
'Every one of those wild fellows,' said I to myself, 'is worth a dozen of the poor mean-spirited book-tramper I have lately been discoursing with.'

But it is not at all clear why Borrow had developed such a feeling of antipathy towards the bookseller.

I too, spoke to a bookseller in Bangor, an elderly resident who, in retirement, now spends his time supplying specialist works on history by mail order. He was a large man with a neatly trimmed white beard and spoke precise English with what some might term a 'cultured accent'. Although he was anxious to tell me something about the books he was selling, I was more interested in his recollections of life in Bangor during the last war.

When Bristol was severely blitzed in 1941 the entertainment department of BBC radio moved to the comparative safety of the city. It was from here that the entertainment output of radio was broadcast that played such a vital role in maintaining morale on the home front during that period.

'At that time we would see all the top entertainers in the streets and shops here,' said the bookseller. 'I often used to chat to Tommy Handley and Jack Train, and Charley Chester would sometimes share a private joke with me.'

He also recalled a dramatic and tragic incident.

'When the Luftwaffe made Liverpool a target for bombing they would often fly along the Caernarfonshire coast. Well there was one occasion when, as a broadcast was going out, a German plane appeared over the Menai Straits pursued by two RAF planes. It had been on a mission to destroy coastal shipping and while it was in this desperate situation the pilot decided to discharge parachute mines. Unfortunately these landed on Bangor, one exploding just outside the broadcasting venue and killing a BBC driver." There is still a recording in existence of that fateful explosion.

Borrow describes a Saturday night at his hotel when

'...the house was thronged with people who had arrived by train from Manchester and Liverpool...'

He complains

'...there was no one with whom I would exchange a thought, or a word of kindness. I addressed several individuals, and in every instance repented...in every countenance near me suspicion, brutality or conceit was most legibly imprinted – I was not amongst the Welsh but the scum of manufacturing England'.

This is a particularly interesting passage, and I know of nothing comparable in any other tourist accounts of Wales. Indeed the reverse perspective can often be found. Many of these sedate travellers tended to consider themselves as quite superior to the Welsh, an extreme colonial attitude which, to some extent, is still with us today. Augusta Pearson, writing in 1853, describes Caernarfon children as 'dirty little Caernarvon brats', while, only two years ago, a 'Sunday Times' journalist made an outrageous attack on the Welsh which was racially motivated.

Chapter Six

CAERNARFON AND SNOWDON

Nowadays we tend to think of Caernarfon as being in the very heartland of Wales, and many Welshmen must feel that it has a more valid claim in many ways to being designated the capital when compared to Cardiff.

Borrow fails to give us any clear impression of the town as it was when he was there, for his principal interest was in its ancient history.

The Roman camp of Segontium was situated there and in the days of resistance it became the outpost of the Welsh stronghold of Eryri.

'It (the town) is called Caernarfon because it is opposite Mona: Caernarfon signifying the town or castle opposite Mona. Its principal feature is its grand old castle, fronting the north and partly surrounded by the sea.'

It is one of the Edwardian castles and therefore its history is inextricably linked to colonialism and the much resented presence of the English monarchy in the creation of the princeship of the country. It is sobering to reflect that this was boosted at one point by a Welshman who is widely regarded as a hero, Lloyd George. As a young man he was the Member of Parliament for Caernarfon and in his role as Chancellor of the Exchequer he stage-managed the 1911 Investiture, assisted by the Bishop of St Asaph at the time.

But there his statue stands today in the town square, near the castle gateway, one arm raised in defiance, his posture suggesting the presence of a born leader. He is addressing an invisible crowd, and gulls come and perch on his shoulder and leave their messes there. The townspeople hardly give him a glance, and if you speak to visiting tourists their total knowledge of this Prime Minister will, frequently, be confined to what they can recall of a television series shown many years ago, in which

Philip Madoc played the lead. Talk to local people and they will tell you previously unheard tales of his youthful sexual prowess.

The town is a busy tourist centre and in 1969 this reached saturation point when the eyes of the world were focused on Caernarfon as the empty razzmatazz of the investiture was enacted. Prince Charles prides himself on his guardianship of our architectural heritage but I am informed that three Georgian houses were demolished in order to provide an enhanced view of him being presented to his subjects.

But despite this political showbiz spectacular – largely devised by that Royal enthusiast Lord Tonypandy, or plain George Thomas as he was then – the language and culture of this part of Wales remain unaffected and there have been commercial gains. It gave the town an even higher profile than it already enjoyed as a tourist centre and the volume of visitors to the castle increased.

The people of Caernarfon seem to take a pride in their Welshness, and this is very evident even on a short visit. Out of season you will hear the Welsh language on all sides.

I fell into conversation with an elderly man, slow speaking and with a strong local accent.

Following a preamble concerning the weather-fine on that particular day as it happened – I asked:

'Do you enjoy living in Caernarfon?'

'Enjoy it!' he exclaimed, 'Do you know, I wouldn't live anywhere else, not for love or money. It's a grand place is Caernarfon...'

'But why do you like it so much?' I interjected.

'Well look around you' he said extending his arms. Then his animation changed quickly to suspicion and he asked 'Anyway, what are these questions in aid of. You could be the bloody tax man as far as I know!'

When I explained that I was a writer gathering material for a book he looked at me blankly.

'Oh, I suppose you're one of those poets are you?'

Our conversation was not getting anywhere and we left him talking in Welsh to another senior citizen, and no doubt their gossip focused on the man who was in town accosting total strangers out of the blue.

* * *

Borrow's highly romantic view of Snowdon typifies that of many other literary tourists in the nineteenth century and no Wales Tourist Board brochure can begin to compare with it!

'Perhaps in the whole world there is no region more picturesquely beautiful than Snowdon, a region of mountains, lakes, cataracts and groves in which Nature shows herself in her most grand and beautiful forms...But it is from its connection with romance that Snowdon derives its chief interest. Who when he thinks of Snowdon does not associate it with the heroes of romance, Arthur and his knights? whose fictitious adventures many of the scenes of which are the valleys and passes of Snowdon, are the origin of romance...'

With the assistance of a guide and accompanied by Henrietta, Borrow ascended Eryri. As they tackled this steep climb he sang a song with 'a fine moral'.

Easy to say 'Behold Eryri',
But difficult to reach its head;
Easy for him whose hopes are cheery
To bid the wretch be comforted.

In 1854 there was only one way in which one could get to the summit and that was to walk up. Nowadays, of course, the sedentary can travel on the mountain railway from Llanberis, although the fare is quite expensive. Passengers have travelled up by rail since 1896 and one cannot help but admire the entire enterprise involved in establishing this line. After all the labourers who were engaged in the construction work had none of the mechanised equipment available today, and they were at the mercy of the elements, the weather being frequently unpredictable.

But Borrow, indomitable walker that he was, may well have frowned on the idea of being transported up a mountain without moving a limb. As he would, perhaps have wished us to, we too walked up, keeping to the side of the railway track all the way. We had no very high expectation of a panoramic view from the top, but our steady, sometimes laborious, footsteps eventually brought us to the highest point in southern Britain. Having walked around for a while we then went into the summit hotel for coffee. When Borrow was there refreshments were served in a

'...rude cabin...in which a person resides throughout the year'.

He later stood

'...enjoying a scene inexpressibly grand, comprehending a considerable part of the mainland of Wales, the whole of Anglesey, a faint glimpse of part of Cumberland; the Irish Channel, and what might be either a misty creation or the shadowy outlines of the hills of Ireland'.

Unfortunately we saw none of this for my assumption concerning the limited visibility had proved all too correct and only the immediate mountain environs were clearly discernible, although a few hundred feet below us it was a fairly fine Autumn day.

Borrow's account of Eryri has been used by more than one anthologist and it includes his dramatic rendering of these verses by Goronwy Owen:

Oer yw'r Eira ar Eryri, – o'ryw
Ar awyr i rewi;
Oer yw'r iâ ar riw'r ri,
A'r Eira oer yw 'Ryri.

O Ri y 'Ryri yw'r oera, – o'r âr,
Ar oror wir arwa;
O'r awyr a yr Eira,
O'i ryw i roi rew a'r iâ.

His translation of these lines are as follows:

Cold is the snow on Snowdon's brow,
It makes the air so chill;
For cold, I trow, there is no snow
Like that on Snowdon's hill.

A hill most chill is Snowdon's hill,
And wintry is his brow;
From Snowdon's hill the breezes chill
Can freeze the very snow.

Inevitably Eryri has inspired many poets over the centuries. In his long poem 'The Prelude', for example, Wordsworth describes a moonlit ascent on a Summer night, the object being to watch dawn break from the summit:

'The moon stood naked in the Heavens, at height
Immense above my head, and on the shore
I found myself of a huge sea of mist,
Which meek and silent rested at my feet'.

John Ceiriog Hughes also recalls watching day break from this high point:

> 'And loud we gave a triple shout
> To hail the new-born day –
> As the morning bright, with crimson light
> The night time drove away:
> We called then for the harper
> And in the morning light
> We sang the song of 'Toriad Dydd'
> On Wyddfa's utmost height'.

Eryri seems so solid a topographical presence that it is difficult to think of it being vulnerable. But within recent decades this vulnerability has given rise to serious concern among conservationists, who claim that the alarming erosion of footpaths is producing problems. The Snowdonia National Park Authority are doing all they can to deal with this situation, which has arisen from the high annual tourist influx to the area. Balancing the National Park guidelines with public enjoyment of the region is by no means easy. Wales needs tourists for its economic survival, but at what cost?

Not all poems about Eryri are rooted in the romantic past and the contemporary problems facing Snowdonia are dealt with by the Anglo-Welsh poet Mike Jenkins. In the poem that follows he uses personification to maximum effect.

Yr Wyddfa Speaks Out!

It's summer again
and trip-trap trailing termites
carrying their backpacks
tread me down
sporting 'I've climbed Snowdon'
T-shirts: who's this 'Snowdon' anyway,
some kind of Lord?

It's rack and pinion all the way
the bumper to bumper
wanderlust like humping Nature
from grassy foothills
to flushes of heather;

get away from city-life
and breathe in fresh steam
laced with red-hot cinders.

Oh! Not again! here comes
the birdwatcher with two black eyes
jutting out, the silly old buzzard
hovering on an edge for hours
in his khaki plumage.

And there's nothing more boring
than a geomorphologist
labelling me with terms
like arrêtes and U-shaped valleys,
as the light changes
he's too busy turning pages.

Look at that snap of photographers
trying to suck the scenery
into those extended noses,
if I had the power to bring fog
swirling around my summit
to confound their art, I'd do it.

Those campers with butterfly nets,
at least they linger
to get moist with the dew
I perspire, try to listen
to my heart whose sounds
fall down to lakes, where my reflection
swims towards another winter.

Borrow's visit took place long before the advent of modern tourism, of
course, and as he descended he would not have met, as we did, workmen
attempting to repair the damage caused by a saturation of walkers.

Eryri has attracted walkers and climbers since the seventeenth
century and the first recorded ascent was by Thomas Johnson the
botanist, in 1639. But it was only in the late eighteenth century that
visitors began to arrive in any significant numbers, although, having said
that, these do not begin to compare with today's onslaught. It was the
Romantic period and artists and poets, including Wordsworth, felt drawn

to this gigantic landmark. Some had read that veteran traveller Thomas Pennant, who hailed from Flintshire, and had a considerable influence on literary and artistic tourism in Wales at that time. In the nineteenth century the numbers of creative visitors to the area had increased, and of course, Borrow enjoys a unique position at the forefront among these.

But today's tourism has produced some curious results and nowadays you can actually buy a small piece of Eryri for £30. We are invited to 'own a miniature estate on Snowdon', consisting of an extremely small area, together with a scroll bearing the owners name. One can, I suppose, understand the appeal of this for Welsh exiles anxious to tell their friends in Patagonia or the United States that they own a portion of Wales.

Llanberis is given only a cursory mention by Borrow; he refers to it as 'a small village'.

It is still a village and the entire area is one which has seen the extremes of historical progression. Close to Llyn Peris is Dolbadarn castle, which was built in a circular shape with hard stone. William Roscoe writing in 1853 described it in these words:

'The seat of feudal violence or revenge, a succession of hapless victims immured within its dungeon often filled the adjacent hills and valleys with cries of distress'.

These included Prince Owain, frequently referred to as Owain Goch, who was held captive by his brother Llywelyn, against whom he was plotting with the younger brother of the family. They were defeated and Owain was condemned to spend twenty years in solitary confinement in the dungeon. During Glyndŵr's lifetime it frequently changed hands, as it was a vital fortification in the heartland of Snowdonia.

Such stories are the stuff which Hollywood films are now made of, and the media have hardly even begun yet to explore the very real potential of this fascinating material.

But at the other historical extreme, the hills around Llanberis are scarred, bearing the ugly features associated with slate quarrying. The very hills which resounded with the cries of conflict at Dolbadarn have also echoed to the sounds of industrial activity as the quarry workers laboured for wages in order to enhance the British economy and line the pockets of their employers.

The history of the industry has been popularised, and it is now possible to see authentically restored workshops in which the machinery and tools used by the workers are on display.

I feel rather ambivalent about the presentation of the Welsh past in this way. Museums of this kind are a growing phenomenon and while this has much to commend it, I cannot help wondering whether Wales may eventually become a series of theme parks. Perhaps there are times when, as a nation, the Welsh put too much emphasis on the past.

Chapter Seven

YNYS MÔN

'I will go to the land of Mona, notwithstanding the water of the Menai, across the sand without waiting for the ebb'.

These are the translated words of a sixteenth century poet and Borrow interpreted them as a prophecy of a time when the Menai would be spanned by a bridge.

'Grounding their hopes upon that couplet people were continually expecting to see a bridge across the Menai; more than two hundred years, however, elapsed before the expectation was fulfilled by the mighty Telford flinging across the strait an iron suspension bridge, which, for grace and beauty, has perhaps no rival in Europe'.

He goes on to extol the enterprise involved in extending the railway system over the straits, across which trains at that time were capable of travelling at fifty miles an hour. He goes on to quote some lines written in the mid-seventeenth century which also seem to foretell the shape of things to come:

'I got up in Mona as soon as twas light,
At nine in old Chester my breakfast I took;
In Ireland I dined, and in Mona, ere night
By the turf fire sat, in my own ingle nook'.

Borrow regarded this as remarkable and comments:

'Truly some old bard in the seventeenth century must in a vision of the second sight have seen the railroad bridge across the Menai, the

Chester train dashing across it and a figure exactly like his seated comfortably in a third-class carriage'.

Today, of course, diesel trains speed across to Ynys Môn at even greater speed and with increased passenger comfort.

But, to add a very sombre note, the suicidal have sometimes ended their lives by jumping from the road bridge. Despite the fact that there is a Samaritans office in Bangor, it is a sad fact that certain people consider themselves beyond any kind of help.

* * *

Borrow described Beaumaris as 'a watering place', and praised the view from the castle encompassing

'...the noble rocky coast of the mainland, the most remarkable feature of which is the gigantic Penmaenmawr, the termination of a range of craggy hills descending from the Snowdon mountains'.

He goes on to compare Beaumaris Bay to the bay of Naples. Praise indeed!

Beaumaris is, to me, one of the finest towns in North Wales. It is a clean town, a community with a very obvious sense of civic pride, which it has retained despite the pressures of tourism. While certain resorts have accepted the worst excesses of tourism, Beaumaris has retained its respectable image, and this has been enhanced within recent years by its excellent annual arts festival.

The castle is another Edwardian fortification, begun in 1295, and the other major feature of historic interest is the famous gaol.

Borrow does not relate any conversations with local people, but if he had he might have told the remarkable story of William Lewis, who died at Beaumaris in 1793. Each morning of his life was devoted to the reading of portions of the scriptures and each evening to the consumption of as many as eight gallons of ale. When he died he weighed forty stone and it was necessary to elevate him out of his home with a specially constructed crane. He was evidently something of an eccentric for he dubbed himself 'the King of Spain'.

Eight years after Borrow's visit Richard Rowlands met a sad fate and was hanged at Beaumaris Gaol, having been accused of the murder of his father-in-law. He insisted that he was completely innocent and prior to his execution barricaded himself in his cell. The governor attempted to reason with him but to no avail. Eventually the prison warders were forced to batter the door down and poor Rowlands was dragged, kicking and shouting, to the place of execution. As the rope was being secured around his neck he continued to protest his innocence, but his final words were by way of a curse. This was directed at the clock of the nearby church, which he claimed would not function normally again after his death. The reason for Rowland's behaviour became clear shortly afterwards when another man confessed to the crime.

Mike Jenkins has a poem about the plight of Richard Rowlands, in which he prepares himself for the inevitable:

'I pace my own funeral – walk daily,
rehearsing the last light, I look down
on a plague of faces below me
drooling because it's not their plight:
I curse time with my pendulous body'.

On the quay I encountered a tall man in his forties, casually dressed and with an expensive camera around his neck. When we exchanged greetings I quickly realised that he was American.

'Is this your first visit to Wales?' I asked.

'Yeah,' he responded, 'and gee it's a real wonderful country. It's really beautiful, and do you know something? There are guys in the States who've never even heard of Wales, or, if they have, they maybe think its a county of England.'

'I can see that the Wales Tourist Board are going to have to work harder' I commented.

He then told me that he lived in Boston and was a television executive.

'Do you know where my paternal great grandfather came from' he exclaimed with a broad smile. 'Its no use me trying to pronounce the place,' he went on, and at this point he produced an ordinance survey map. 'Look, I'll show you on this.'

He pointed to Harlech.

'He was some kind of shepherd, I'm told. Isn't that something?'

I agreed that it was, and at the end of our chat we shook hands warmly.

'Enjoy the rest of your visit to Wales' I said.

'I sure will,' came the enthusiastic response. 'And I'll be back, make no mistake about that!'

* * *

Writing in the early eighteenth century Daniel Defoe had observed

> 'There is nothing of note to be seen in the isle of Anglesey but the castle of Beaumaris...'

Subsequent travellers have found much of interest to write about in the region and Borrow was no exception.

His main reason for wishing to visit Ynys Môn derived from his deep interest in the work of Goronwy Owen, and at the time he would probably have been the only Englishman able to read and appreciate the work of this poet.

He wished to see the home of this revered figure, and the landscape which moved him to such an intense sense of hiraeth when he was living in exile in America.

> 'Great is my grief for her,
> Ynys Môn is like Zion to me;
> My life will not be comforted
> Without Ynys Môn, despite every song or chord'.

Goronwy Owen was born at Dafarn Goch at Llanfair Mathafan Eithaf in 1723, and his family had been tinkers. He displayed early scholastic brilliance and became one of the most illustrious pupils at Friars School in Bangor, and from there he secured a place at Jesus College, Oxford. Eventually he became a cleric and served his native parish, but because of an unfair decision by the clerical authorities his stay was short lived. Although he hoped for another parish in Wales this failed to materialise. Eventually he was offered a teaching post at a grammar school in Virginia and emigrated with his family in 1757. Tragedy struck when both his wife and younger child died during the voyage. After a time he married again in America, but his second wife also died prematurely. As a result of these personal tragedies Owen turned to the consolation of alcohol and this began to affect his working life, and it was not long before he was dismissed. His resilience enabled him to pick up the threads and he married yet again. The final decade of his life was spent as vicar of a parish in Virginia. He himself died in 1769 and was buried on a tobacco plantation which he owned near Lawrenceville.

'He was the last of the great poets of Cambria,' enthused Borrow, 'and with the exception of ap Gwilym the greatest she has produced.'

In order to pursue his literary pilgrimage Borrow walked in very warm weather through a landscape which, with the exception of subsequent houses and farms and twentieth century roads, must today be much the same as it was a hundred and fifty years ago.

Borrow described Llanfair Mathafan Eithaf as 'a depressing place' complaining that '...hogs came about me grunting and sniffing'.

He paid a visit to the churchyard in the hope of discovering inscriptions on tombstones relating to Owen's family. He was accompanied by a local man, a miller. When this guide referred at one point to a nearby building which, apparently, had once been a monastery, but had since been converted into a farmhouse, Borrow made sectarian capital out of this:

'May all monasteries be converted into farm houses and may they still retain their original names in mockery of Popery'.

When, a little further on, he came across a half erected house and addressed one of the workmen in Welsh, Borrow was more than a little surprised when the man replied in Spanish. When asked how he had acquired the language he explained:

'I have been in Chili, sir, and in California, and in those places I learned Spanish.'
'What did you go to Chili for?' said I.
'I went there as a mariner' said the man.

Borrow naturally wondered why this native of Ynys Môn should have spoken to him in Spanish instead of in his native language.

'Why, I saw it was not your language, sir, and as I had picked up some Spanish I thought it would be but fair to answer you in it'.

The inherent implication here is that Borrow's spoken Welsh was imperfect, at least on this occasion.

The building on which the man was working became the California Inn. In 1974 the man's grandson, Gwilym Jones, was interviewed by the BBC. He revealed that after his grandfather had ceased to be a mariner he returned to Ynys Môn and bought a sailing boat. He also became a member of a Methodist chapel and presented a large and very fine Bible for the pulpit readings. However, he was caught smuggling salt to Red Wharf Bay and fined at Beaumaris. His fellow members at the chapel took an extremely dim view of this misdemeanour and removed the privilege of membership. By way of protest, during a morning service, he walked to the pulpit, and recovered the Bible. As he walked out of the chapel with it the moralistic deacons must have been astonished!

We tend to assume that people living in North Wales in the nineteenth century were not widely travelled. Although this is certainly true up to a point, we should not forget the men who were given the opportunity to see other shores either through their enlistment in the army or the navy, or in their involvement in colonial trade, often in very menial ways.

Gwilym Jones, himself, had also been to sea, having signed on in 1925. He recalled, in the interview, the conditions on a tramp-steamer at that time, when the men would be on duty for up to eighty-four hours a week, four on and four off. As the ice box was only capable of carrying enough food for nine days the meals were usually of very poor quality.

Borrow also revealed that a local innkeeper named Pritchard had also travelled extensively, having been to Constantinople and Alexandria among other places.

Pritchard's daughter at this inn, at Pentraeth Coch, is described by Borrow as 'a buxom damsel'. She was capable of conversing with equal fluency in both Welsh and English:

'Which language do you prefer?' said I.
'I think I like the English best,' said the girl, 'it is the most useful language.'
'Not in Anglesey' said I.
'Well,' said the girl, 'it is the most genteel.'
'Gentility,' said I, 'will be the ruin of Welsh, as it has been of many other things...'

The girl's muddled attitude was possibly not uncommon in the Wales of that period, and to some measure this may have been due to the influence of both the Anglican church and the existence of influential local squirearchies – English landowners who, by and large, had little or no interest in the Welsh and their life and culture. The attitude of some of these may well have been summed up by the literary critic and poet Mathew Arnold. He was firmly of the opinion that

'...if a Welshman has anything of real importance to say he must say it in English'.

When Borrow finally arrived at the home of Goronwy Owen he found an extremely humble dwelling occupied by a woman and several children. When he engaged this woman in conversation, explaining the object of his visit, she made it clear that she preferred to communicate with him through a third party who could act as an interpreter. A neighbour fulfilled this function, and, writes Borrow,

'...she could understand his way of speaking much better than mine'.

Is this a further reflection on the possible limitations of Borrow's spoken Welsh?

Through this man he is able to enquire whether the children are descendants of Goronwy:

'She pointed to the children and said that they had all some of his blood. I asked in what relationship they stood to Goronwy. She said she could hardly tell, that three marriages stood between them, and that the relationship was on the mother's side'.

Borrow was particularly taken with one of the children, a little girl, and the woman informed him that her name was Ellen. This led Borrow to what we may regard as a remarkably naive assumption:

'...I had no doubt that the children were related to the illustrious Goronwy. Ellen is a very uncommon Welsh name, but it seems to have been a family name of the Owen's'.

Ellen, in fact, was a quite common Christian name for Welsh children in Victorian times, but despite this Borrow creates the impression that he has made an important discovery.

Back at the inn at Pentraeth Borrow fell into a revealing conversation with a man with the Dickensian sounding name, Mr Bos.

Bos, despite his name, is a native of Ynys Môn, and when he learned that Borrow has visited Llanfair he remarked that he

'...can't conceive how any person could have any business in Anglesey save that business be pigs or cattle'.

When Borrow explained that he has been to see

'...the birthplace of a great man – the cleverest Anglesey ever produced'

he is taken to task by Bos, who tells him that he should have gone to Penmynydd, where Owain Tudur was born.

Bos went on to explain that he had been able to pick up a knowledge of history through six months schooling at Beaumaris and by what he had been told in moving around the country in the course of his work. When Borrow asked him about the nature of his work he learned that he was a drover, to which he reacted with disdain:

'Pray excuse me, but is not droving rather a low-lifed occupation'.

He went on to add further fuel to the fire by being overtly vindictive

'...When I asked you that question about droving I merely did so because one Ellis Wynne, in a book he wrote, gives the drovers a very bad character, and puts them in Hell for their malpractices'.

It becomes obvious that the poorly educated Bos had not heard of Ellis Wynne, although he knew a dealer in pigs of the same name. The misunderstanding leads to a spirit of revenge and Bos vows that the next time he meets him in Corwen he will 'crack his head'. He continues:

'...Written a book has he? Then I suppose he has been left a legacy, and gone to school after middle-age, for when I last saw him he could neither read nor write'.

This seems to be a further example of Borrow taking advantage of an encounter in which the other person has neither the education nor the personality to compete on an equal basis.

Bos later talks about

'...the comparative merits of Anglesey runts and Scotch bullocks'.

In the same sentence he goes on to compare the women of Northampton, to which his travels have taken him, and the women of Wrexham.

It almost goes without saying that nowadays this would be regarded as extremely politically incorrect and would, doubtless produce a heated reaction not only among the feminists but among women in general.

When on his way to Penmynydd Borrow met a local and asked him the name of a nearby hill. He was told that it is called Moelfre, and reflected

'...I little thought when I was looking from the road near Pentraeth Coch yesterday, and admiring the tranquillity that I was gazing upon the scene of one of the most tremendous conflicts in history or poetry'.

The combatants consisted of men who supported Owain Gwynedd and the united forces of the Irish Locklanders and Normans.

Borrow explained what happened to the local in graphic terms:

'...according to the words of a poet, who described it, the Menai could not ebb on account of the torrent of blood which flowed into it, slaughter was heaped upon slaughter, shout followed shout and around Moelfre a thousand war flags waved'.

There is an incidental reference to Madog, who traditionally has been regarded as Owain Gwynedd's son. However some historians now take the view that there may not have been a blood relationship between them at all.

Madog is best known as the Welshman who discovered America. Understandably, there have been difficulties involved in proving this claim, and his name has been much overshadowed by that of Columbus. There is little doubt that Madog did sail to the New World, landing at Mobile Bay in about 1169, but whether he was the first European to reach that continent is now open to considerable doubt. If, as seems likely, someone else arrived before him, then, in one sense at least, it does not matter too much. For many in Wales it is still a cherished myth, and by means of myths the Welsh are able to define and redefine their nationality and identity.

* * *

Bread of the wholesomest is found
In my mother land of Anglesey:
Friendly bounteous men abound
In Penymynnydd of Anglesey.

Our veteran traveller sang these words, written by a bard named Robin Ddu, as he entered

'...a small village consisting of a few white houses and a mill...The meaning of Penymynnydd is literally top of a hill...'

Borrow visited the church and he found a very willing guide in a pretty servant girl from the nearby parsonage. When inside the church he asked the girl which of the tombs was that of Owain Tudur and his wife.

' "There it is, sir," said she, pointing to the north side of the church, "there is the tomb of Owain Tudur".
Beneath a low-roofed arch lay sculptured in stone, on an altar tomb, the figure of a man and woman; that of the man in armour; that of the woman in graceful drapery'. .

But Borrow already knew that this could not possibly be the tomb of Owain Tudur and his wife and claims that

'I was unwilling to dispel a pleasing delusion'.

In the War of the Roses Owain was a Lancastrian, but was taken prisoner at the Battle of Mortimer's Cross and executed at Hereford. As he rested his head on the block and awaited the axe to be wielded he told the executioner

'Be tender to my head. It hath lain in the lap of a Queen'.

His wife was the widow of Henry V.

* * *

It is a peculiarity among nineteenth century writers that frequently they merely hinted at the names of certain places or people. I am unable to fathom why Borrow should refer to Llangefni as L –, as though by revealing its name some vital secret will be exposed.
     When he arrived at Llangefni – "a small neat town" – the chapter covering the visit is taken up with a description of his experiences at the inn at which he sought refreshment. He was under the impression that in eating and drinking at this particular inn he was patronising a local poet, whom he mistakenly thought owned it. When he discovered his mistake he exclaimed:

'Here was a pretty affair! I had entered the house and ordered the chop and pint in the belief that by so doing I was patronising the poet, and lo, I was not in the poet's house, and my order would benefit a person for whom, however respectable and religious, I care not one rush'.

His bad temper was added to when he is served not with ale but with sherry

'...for which I have always entertained a sovereign contempt, as a silly, sickly compound, the use of which will transform a nation, however bold and warlike by nature, into a race of sketchers, scribblers and punsters, in fact into what Englishmen are at the present day'.

Our visit to Llangefni was a more pleasant one than Borrow's, and it gave us the opportunity to call on a friend, Chas Parry Jones. He is a former general practitioner and we were able to catch up on our news over lunch in his spacious house in Glan Hwfa Road. Chas is also a poet and literary enthusiast, and some of our gossip was about literary matters. He has a quite remarkably wide network of friends and acquaintances throughout North Wales, and after we left him I reflected, yet again, on what a small country Wales in general is. Mention the name of someone living in, say, Ruthin or Ffestiniog and this can ring bells for someone else living in Carmarthen or Builth Wells:

'Oh yes, I met him once. My brother was at college with him'.
'He told me he'd served with Dad in the army once. Great bloke.'
'Oh. Amazing you should mention her. She's a cousin of mine!'

To the outside world this may appear like insularity, but surely it gives the Welsh a valuable sense of kinship in a country which, despite its physical smallness, is big in terms of interpersonal relationships. At a time when outside Wales the trend is moving increasingly towards the impersonal, it is good that the Welsh can relate to each other in these terms.

The people are very friendly at Llangefni – as indeed they are in Ynys Môn as a whole – and the Welsh language seems to be alive and well there.

I recalled that when John Wesley had visited Llangefni in 1748 he had written in a strange way about what he interpreted as linguistic alienation. He went to a religious service:

'...we understood little of what we heard. Oh what a heavy curse was the Confusion of Tongues! And how grievous are the effects of it! All the birds of the air, all the beasts of the field, understand the language of their own species. Man only is a barbarian to man, unintelligible to his own brethren'.

This is clearly a very curious observation, for Wesley appears to find it difficult to accept the fact that our world is made up of a rich diversity of languages, all of which define nationality and culture.

Llangefni has a fine purpose built art gallery in Oriel Ynys Môn, situated on the edge of the town. Knowing that there was an important retrospective exhibition of works by Kyffin Williams on display we lost little time in finding the gallery, and spent a most interesting hour there.

If one of the marks of genius lies in the presence of an unmistakable stamp on an art work then Kyffin Williams has it in abundance. His work could not be taken for that of any of his contemporaries and he has rejected the cosy pastoral landscape in favour of an evocation of North Wales which is characterised by things as they actually are, neither more nor less.

He lives on the shores of the Menai Straits and, in his late seventies now, is as prolific as he ever was.

* * *

Proceeding on his journey Borrow found the countryside

'...poor and mean – on my right was a field of oats, on my left a Methodist chapel – oats and Methodism! What better symbols of poverty and meanness'.

His dislike of Methodism was rivalled only by his hatred of Catholicism. A dogmatic unrelenting low-church Anglican he was not prepared to open his mind in order to tolerate either the faith of other denominations, or certain of the adherents of these beliefs.

He observed a house which

'...exhibited an appearance of great desolation...a white, or rather grey, structure of some antiquity'.

Two men were standing outside and one of these informed Borrow that the house was called Ty Gwyn. Clearly this man found Borrow's manner of conversational Welsh rather curious for he commented to his neighbour

'...though he speaks Welsh, his Welsh sounds very different from ours'.

We have to remember, of course, that, for all his linguistic ability, Borrow would probably have spoken with a fairly pronounced Norfolk accent, so it is, perhaps, inevitable that some should find him difficult to converse with.

He was told that Ty Gwyn was owned by a Mr Sparrow from Liverpool, and one of the men was employed as a bailiff. He told Borrow of the tendency, even in 1854, for Englishmen to buy land and property in Wales, something which some of us may regard as a fairly recent development.

'...the lands are almost entirely taken possession of by Saxons. Wherever you go you will find them settled, and a Saxon bird of the roof must build its nest at Ty Gwyn'

Nowadays, of course, the English presence on Ynys Môn consists primarily of those who have moved there to live on a permanent basis, often retired people, those owning second homes on the island, and those who come on holiday during the summer months.

There are certain passages in 'Wild Wales' which are, intentionally or unintentionally, amusing, but personally I find it difficult to decide which. Take this conversation, for example, one of the funniest in the entire book, which also occurs while he is questioning the two men at Ty Gwyn:

'Have you any memorials in the neighbourhood of the old Welsh?' said I.
'What do you mean?' said the man in the cap.
'Any altars of the Druids?' said I, pointing to some stones which had struck my attention.
'Mere common rocks' said the man.
'May I go and examine them?' said I.
'O yes,' said he of the hat, 'and we will go with you.'
We went to the stones which were indeed common rocks...'

On this occasion the antiquarian side of Borrow's nature was a little over-zealous!

Later in the conversation he exclaims proudly that he is a man of Norfolk

'...where the people eat the best dumplings in the world, and speak the purest English'.

In spite of his denigratory comments at various other points in the book concerning the Saxons in general, he was evidently a passionate chauvinist where his own region is concerned.

When he was close to Holyhead night was drawing in, and he was overtaken by a train travelling at speed along the nearby line:

"I despise railroads" said I, "and those who travel by them." When he eventually arrived at his destination he was not favourably impressed:

"...I found myself in the midst of a poor, dull, ill-lighted town".

Having secured accommodation close to the railway terminus, Borrow was content to rest in the comfortable coffee-room. He asked that the servant who specialised in cleaning boots be brought to him. 'The boots' is a

'...grey haired venerable man...'

to whom Borrow revealed, in an incidental way, that he is

'...fond of poetry, and takes especial delight in inspecting the birth places and haunts of poets'.

It quickly emerged that the 'boots' is no uneducated servant, but someone who was not only knowledgeable about the works of Goronwy Owen and other poets, but a poet himself:

'Ah, if your honour is fond of poets and their places you did right to come to Anglesey – and your honour was right in saying that you can't stir a step without meeting one; you have an example of the truth of that in me – for to tell your honour the truth, I am a poet myself'.

It is still the case nowadays that poets may be met with quite unexpectedly in Wales and as often as not they may be working in areas quite unrelated to the arts. For example, many years ago, in the sixties, the then Third Programme of BBC radio broadcast a superb verse play based on the life of the Spanish poet Lorca. Quite by chance, a couple of years after hearing the play, I met the author, Dai Richards, in what might seem to some an unlikely setting. He was working as a labourer on a housing development project at Harlech.

Poetry in Wales matters in a way which it will probably never do in England, where it tends to be treated as 'literary' or even 'academic', with all which that may imply for some people. But the poet this side of Offa's Dyke can be seen in a completely different context, and this is probably due to some extent to historical factors.

In the middle ages Welsh poets were regarded as important, and a prospective bard would be trained and only admitted into the ranks of the most reputable after attaining very high standards. The legacy of this tradition has resulted, along with other factors, in a vibrant literary culture today.

Having enjoyed a refreshing night's sleep at the Railway Hotel, Borrow set out to see Caer Gybi, and has a few comments to make about the saint.

Gybi, he tells us, was

'...a great walker and from bronzing his countenance by frequent walking in the sun, was generally called Cybi Velin, which means tawny or yellow Cybi'.

Our traveller strolled down to the breakwater and pier at the mouth of the harbour, where he encountered some Irish reapers. They were resting idly with their backs against a wall and speaking in Irish. When they became aware of Borrow's presence they began to get to their feet and he became the object of their attention:

'All the Irish were looking at me – presently they formed into knots, and began to discourse very eagerly'.

One of them, acting as a spokesman for the others, approached Borrow and it quickly became evident that he had been mistaken for, of all things, a Catholic priest named Toban.

This group were awaiting the next sailing for Ireland, and their spokesman requested that Father Toban should give them his blessing for the voyage.

Nothing which Borrow tells them will convince these men that he is not the person they have taken him for, and his protestations are worthy of inclusion in any anthology of Victorian comic writing. Here is a brief sample:

'But suppose I refuse?'
'Why in such a case, we should just make bound to give your reverence a good bating.'
'Kill me?'
'We would, your reverence.'

In the end this dyed-in-the wool Anglican is forced into granting a blessing to these Catholic peasants:

'...there knelt thirty bare-headed Eirionaich on the pier at Caer Gybi, beneath the broiling sun. I gave them the best Latin blessing I could remember out of two or three which I had got by memory out of an old Popish book of devotion'.

Whether this is an absolutely true account of what happened, or whether Borrow was greatly exaggerating what may have been a more minor misunderstanding, it is impossible to tell, and it doesn't matter very much anyway, in a sense, as it makes such a delightful story.

Borrow's initial rather unfavourable impression of Holyhead was reversed when he saw it in daylight. He wrote of

'...a town with its white houses placed by the seaside, on the skirt of a mountain, beneath a blue sky'.

Holyhead's main claim to fame is, of course, its port, and all traffic bound for Dublin travels through the middle of Ynys Môn in order to board the very frequent ferry service.

In 1727 Jonathan Swift was on his way from London to Dublin when his sailing was delayed due to bad weather. Never the most easy of men to please, he was forced to kill time in an inn, where he wrote these lines:

'Lo here I sit at Holy Head
With muddy ale and mouldy bread
All Christian victuals stink of fish
I'm where my enemies would wish'.

Historically, as one would expect, the town is steeped in tales of the sea, while only a few miles away it is air-power which has pride of place at the RAF base at Valley. During the last war many servicemen, including Americans, took off from Valley for bombing missions over Hitler's

Germany, but sadly, as we know, so many did not return.

Holyhead today is, in general, a fairly unremarkable town, and regrettably, the focal point, the town centre, has met with the fate of a number of other towns in North Wales. They have been pedestrianised, and the total visual effect of black bollards, together with the replacement of traditional stone pavements with unattractive tiles, is quite at variance with the original design of these communities. The character and atmosphere of some of our older Welsh towns has been ripped away in this process. Obviously the problem of traffic in urban centres had to be dealt with but I cannot help feeling that other less radical options might have been considered.

Possibly the jewel in Holyhead's crown today is Canolfan Ucheldre, the arts centre. This was established in 1991 due to the unstinting initiative of a group of local people, including the well known lexicographer David Crystal. One of the staff Sue Jones, explained that the building had previously been a convent boarding and day school run by an order of French nuns, 'Le Bon Sauveur'. The school chapel is now the main hall of the arts complex and the only original part remaining. A sympathetic addition has been made to this building, housing an exhibition hall, a shop and restaurant.

The centre has its own repertory company and their productions are far from run-of-the-mill. Sue told me that they would be staging 'The Merchant of Venice' later in the year.

Back at his hotel Borrow sought the advice of the ever-helpful literary 'boots' concerning the best route to take back to Bangor. However, he reflected that

'...if I followed his advice I should not see the north side of the island nor its principal town Amlwch, and received for answer that if I never did, the loss would not be great'.

To my mind this is applicable to Amlwch as it exists today, and whenever, out of necessity, I have to make a stop there I am always thankful to move on again. The entire town appears to have a grey uniformity about it which I find depressing. The contrast with, say, Beaumaris could not be greater.

In company with a nephew of the 'boots', who acted as his guide, Borrow ascended Pen Caer Gybi. On reaching the summit he was suitably impressed:

'The prospect, on every side, was noble: the blue interminable sea to the west and north; the whole stretch of Mona to the east: and far away to the south the mountainous region of Eryri, comprising some of the most romantic hills in the world'.

He has surprisingly little to say about the South Stack lighthouse, which, of course, was then manually controlled. He merely refers to

'...a lighthouse standing on the verge of a precipice, the foot of which was washed by the sea'.

When I was a schoolboy it was manually operated and I recall being shown around by a keeper. Nowadays all the lighthouses along the British coastline are automatically controlled, of course, and what must have been an extremely lonely job has gone for ever.

But at least in following in our traveller's footsteps I was able to descend down a seemingly unending flight of steps to enable me to obtain a closer view of the lighthouse. As I got nearer to the lower reaches the sea was pounding relentlessly against the rugged rocks below.

On the day following his visit to South Stack, and against his better judgement, Borrow took the advice of the 'boots' and took a train back to Bangor, the only occasion on his tour when he resorted to wheels.

* * *

'...one whose memory haunted me much more than that of Cybi during my stay in Holyhead'.

This is part of Borrow's eulogistic summary of the achievement of the poet Lewis Morris, who should not be confused with a nineteenth century poet of the same name from Carmarthenshire.

Although our traveller did not visit any of the places associated with Morris on the island – his birthplace for example – he does devote approximately two pages to his life and work. He was one of a celebrated island family and was born in 1701. As a young man he developed much skill in land surveying and this eventually resulted in work on the first properly surveyed chart of the Welsh coastline. In 1742 he moved to Aberystwyth where he began to take a great interest in lead mining. Eventually he worked at Aberdyfi as a collector of customs and never returned to Ynys Môn.

His immense interest in the native literature of Wales led to his invaluable contribution to a revival of interest in the work of the poets at a time of cultural crisis. This was brought about by the tendency of patrons to be attracted increasingly not by the Welsh-language poets, whom they had previously assisted, but by those writing in English; there was no Arts Council in those days!

But Morris' own literary works were prolific, and, in general terms, the best way of defining his greatness is to describe him as a polymath.

Borrow sums up his achievement by quoting Goronwy Owen:

'As long as Bardic lore shall last, science and learning be cherished, the language and blood of the Britons undefiled, song be heard on Parnassus, heaven and earth be in existence, foam be on the surge, and water in the river, the name of Lewis of Môn shall be held in grateful remembrance'.

* * *

When it comes to holidays I fail to respond to the promises of glossy brochures which go into raptures about exotic, sun-drenched locations. While many of my acquaintances are happy to fly out to the Greek islands or Barbados I prefer to visit Ireland or Brittany. But each year I also enjoy what some may regard as a 'busman's holiday' for a North Walian, a stay on Ynys Môn.

Pamela and I rent a traditional whitewashed cottage a mile or so from Llanfaethlu and there we while away halcyon days walking for miles along the coast, exploring the beaches and coves, watching the bird life and taking photographs. When we are feeling more sedentary we sit in the garden and watch the ferry boats sailing to, and leaving, Holyhead, some nine miles away. At night we are able to watch the flashing light of the Skerries lighthouse close to Carmel Head.

Although Borrow does not record visiting this particular area of the island, while retracing his steps we spent four nights at Llanfaethlu staying in the cottage.

Leaving on a Tuesday morning we headed across the island towards Llanfairpwll, where I had an appointment with someone whose name is synonymous with the region, the broadcaster and journalist Ian Skidmore. Arrangements had been made for me to record a half-hour radio programme at his home. As we sat in his book-lined study, with a producer recording our conversation in the next room, we exchanged some literary gossip. At one point Borrow was mentioned briefly, and, with characteristic frankness, Ian expressed an extremely ambivalent attitude. " 'Wild Wales' is a great book, the first travel book I ever read about Wales," he exclaimed. "But I loathe and detest Borrow!"

We have a curious anomaly here, for although 'Wild Wales' is so readable the personality of the author is such that he is hardly the kind of person one might be particularly anxious to meet!

Chapter Eight

FELINHELI – BEDDGELERT – FFESTINIOG

When Borrow arrived back in Bangor he spent a further night there, and on the next day continued his journey. He found himself in Felinheli (Port Dinorwig) which at that time consisted of only a hundred houses). When he entered an inn he fell into conversation with two men who were discussing that fascinating marine creature the serpent. Borrow took some satisfaction in relating a tale which, although it concerned a local happening, he assumed they would not know about:

'Once in October in the year 1805 as a small vessel of the Traeth was upon the Menai, sailing very slowly, the weather being very calm, the people on board saw a strange creature like an immense worm swimming after them. It soon overtook them, climbed on board through the tiller-hole, and coiled itself on the deck under the mast – the people at first were dreadfully frightened, but taking courage they attacked it with an oar and drove it overboard...'

We will encounter a further creature of the deep in a later chapter, when we arrive in Bala.

As their conversation continues Borrow is told by one of the men

'...you are of South Wales – your Welsh is very different from ours'.

He responded with a further quip about his Englishness:

'I am not of South Wales. I am the seed not of the sea-snake but of the coiling serpent, for so one of the old Welsh poets called the Saxons'.

The growth of Felinheli as a significant port in the nineteenth century is inextricably linked to the expansion of slate quarrying in Caernarfonshire. From there slate was exported to other countries, where it was used extensively. But as quarrying declined the port began to loose its former importance, and nowadays it is a place which might not appear to be particularly appealing unless you have an interest in its history and have read Reg Chambers Jones' very readable account of its development and decline.

Although Felinheli is not a place which really figures on the tourist map of Wales, on the day on which we were there a party of pensioners from St Helens had just arrived in a coach.

I spoke to one of them, a rotund, ruddy faced, man in his seventies.

When I commented that it was good to see so many Autumn visitors in Wales, he replied: 'We ain't all fair-weather folks you know, us oldies. We ain't afraid of a drop of rain or a bit of cold'.

'But of course not,' I quickly and apologetically responded. 'But what do you think of this part of Wales?'

'Wales is a grand place,' he replied, 'I used to go every year to stay at me' daughter's in Rhyl, but now her and her 'usband 'av moved to Birmingham, so I don't get those 'olidays by the sea no more.'

* * *

After leaving Felinheli our traveller returned to Caernarfon. Having refreshed himself in the Castle Inn he set out for Beddgelert. Within less than two hours he was once again

'drawing nigh to the mountainous district of Eryri'.

After a period of walking, which he describes in romanticised terms, he eventually found himself at Llyn Cwellyn. Here he met the Snowdon Ranger and his son-in-law. The younger man, who was a miner, explained:

'A ranger means a guide, sir. My father-in-law is generally termed the Snowdon Ranger because he is a tip-top guide, and he has named the house after him the Snowdon Ranger. He entertains gentlemen in it who put themselves under his guidance in order to ascend Snowdon and see the country'.

Borrow then commented on the inherent occupational risks which both men faced in the course of their daily lives, one from the possibility of a fall from a considerable height, and the other from the possibility of an accident underground.

The Snowdon Ranger inn, beside Llyn Cwellyn, was named after John Morton, the first guide to the summit from this particular side of the mountain. In 1940 the building was acquired as a youth hostel. The derivation of the term Snowdon Ranger, which is also the name of an ascent route, has its origin in Elizabethan times when Snowdonia was a royal forest, and the Queens' favourite Robert Dudley was put in overall charge and assumed the title of Ranger.

When he arrived at Beddgelert, Borrow was thrown into what he clearly regarded as disagreeable company at the inn at which he had decided to stay. He devotes the entire space of a chapter in order to describe his fellow guests. He appears to relish this pen portraiture, and we read, for example, of a 'military puppy' whom he goes on to describe as

'...a tallish fellow, who, though upwards of thirty, affected the airs of a languishing girl, and would fain have made people believe that he was dying of ennui and lassitude'.

He goes on to describe another guest as

'...a creature to do justice to whose appearance would require the pencil of a Hogarth...His countenance was cadaverous, and was eternally agitated by something between a grin and a simper'.

The reader may be forgiven on an occasion like this for feeling that there may well have been occasions when Borrow was determined to discover the most negative of human traits to the exclusion of the more positive qualities which, after all, most people have. A prime example was mentioned in my opening chapter when he encountered a coloured man in Chester.

Borrow may have been taken in by the story of the Llangollen church cat but, thankfully, he was not deceived by the legend surrounding the so-called dog's grave in Beddgelert; he found the legend '...beautiful and affecting' though.

Although the story is very well known in the folklore heritage of Wales, and now figures on teatowels and other tourist artefacts, I make no apology for relating it again here.

The story relates how Llywelyn, Prince of Gwynedd, set out one day from his palace for a days' hunting. He left his infant son with his faithful hound Gelert. On his return he found that the cot was empty. Let the nineteenth century ballad writer William Spencer continue the tale:

O'erturned his infant's bed he found
With bloodstained covert rent
And all around, the walls and ground
With recent blood bespent.

He called his child, no voice repl'd
He searched with terror wild
Blood, blood he found on every side
But nowhere found his child.

'Hell hound! my child's by thee devoured'
The frantic father cry'd
And to the hilt his vengeful sword
He plunged in Gelert's side.

The dog's dying bellow is answered by the cries of the infant, who is alive and uninjured. Shortly afterwards Llewelyn came upon the body of a large wolf and was consumed by remorse. His son's life had been saved by the brave hound. Llywelyn never smiled again.

Vain vain was Llywelyn's woe.
Best of thy kind, adieu,
The frantic blow which laid you low
This head shall ever rue.

Although the origin of the legend will be found much earlier than the eighteenth century, it owes its phenomenal fame due to the dubious efforts of an innkeeper of that period to lure gullible tourists to the village by perpetuating what he claimed was a completely authentic story. If evidence was needed then what better evidence than the grave of Gelert, which is situated in a field a short walk from the village! But this memorial, which is visited by hundreds of people each year, is, possibly, the ultimate in hoaxes of this kind. Today's tourist would no doubt regard Borrow's sentiments at the grave as rather quaint:

'Who is there acquainted with the legend, whether he believes that the dog lies beneath those stones or not, can visit them without exclaiming, with a sigh, "Poor Gelert" '.

In the summer months Beddgelert depends on tourism for its well being but this has not had an adverse effect on the essentially Welsh character of the village, and the surrounding hills retain their strong appeal for the hill walker. Borrow summed up the area in these words:

'Truly the valley of Gelert is a wondrous valley – rivalling for grandeur and beauty any vale either in the Alps or Pyrenees'.

* * *

On his journey from Beddgelert to Ffestiniog, Borrow attempted to take a short cut, but got himself lost and eventually ended up in Maentwrog, where he sought refreshment at the Grapes Inn.

Eventually, by asking directions, he did manage to find Ffestiniog, but he had to stride through a rocky wilderness to do so, and as he did so his thoughts turned to a local bard Rhys Goch, a partisan of Owain Glyndŵr. Borrow

'...repeated stanzas of furious war songs of his, exciting his countrymen to exterminate the English'.

We are also told that Rhys lived to an immense age. An earlier traveller to the same area, George Lyttleton, writing in 1774, was impressed by the general longevity of the local population:

'If you have a mind to live long and renew your youth, come and settle in Ffestiniog. Not long ago there died in that neighbourhood an honest farmer who was 106 years of age. By his first wife he had thirty children, ten by the second, four by the third, and was saved by two concubines...'

For the observant visitor a cafe provides as good a barometer of local rural opinion as any. I sat in a nondescript cafe at Blaenau Ffestiniog and gazed around at the other mid-morning occupants. In one corner was a sandy-headed man in his thirties with a pasty complexion wearing blue, oil-stained overalls; at the next table were two giggling girls in their late teens – one pretty, one plain-dressed uniformly in much worn jeans, split at the knee, and plastic shoes; while at the table near the door was a dark suited serious-looking man with glasses, with a document case at his feet, who, I guessed, was probably a rep for some company or other.

Behind the counter was a dark featured, tall man in a checked shirt who spoke with the distinctive Caernarfonshire accent. I asked him about the employment situation locally and about the plight of young people.

'Well, its the same as everywhere else, isn't it?' he replied. 'There is no work. I feel really sorry for today's youngsters with no prospect of work. This government doesn't seem to be doing anything to help them, does it?'

I agreed with him, and as our conversation continued it focused on the uncaring nature of central government.

'All they're interested in,' said the cafe proprietor, 'is lining their own bloody pockets. I'm all right Jack just about says it all!'

Despite going out of his way to get there Borrow has little of any interest to tell us about Ffestiniog. He makes much of the fact that he believes he has been overcharged for accommodation at his inn, and is displeased by the fact that a local man is unable to enlighten him about a rocky chair on a hillside associated with Rhys Goch.

He also devotes over a page to a book by Walter Scott discovered at his inn, but this has nothing at all to do with either Ffestiniog or Wales in general.

In his tramp from Ffestiniog to Bala Borrow passed through one of the most rugged and remote areas of Wales, and one which, certainly, for my generation, carries poignant echoes of conflict and defeat. I am not referring to an event in the distant historical past but am going back only four decades, to the nineteen-sixties. Tryweryn is a name which is deeply embedded in the Welsh consciousness, and the decision to submerge the farming community of Capel Celyn in order to provide Liverpool Corporation with water can only be described as iniquitous. It grew into a burning issue which not only forced the nationalist front to close ranks but also brought opposition from members of parliament and others who normally distanced themselves from Plaid Cymru. But, once again, English imperialism won the day and Capel Celyn now lies under the still waters of Llyn Celyn reservoir.

'...some ages will elapse before the Welsh forget that the English have conquered them' wrote Borrow over a hundred years before Tryweryn.

Chapter Nine

BALA – LLANGOLLEN AGAIN – RUABON

When Borrow was at Bala no one informed him of anything mysterious under the still waters of Llyn Tegid. But, like Loch Ness, the lake is said to have its monster and this revelation has hit the headlines – 'Monster buffs and boffins could bring boom to Bala' the "Cambrian News" proclaimed – and it has become affectionately known as Teggie. Research scientists and a Japanese television crew are among those who have journeyed to Bala in search of this mysterious creature. In the nineteen seventies a lake warden saw Teggie and described it as being some eight feet in length.

But how did Llyn Tegid come to be where it is? There is a lovely story about this.

On clear moonlit nights, it is said, it is possible to see an old palace under the water of the lake, the palace of a prince, which became submerged because of his failure to heed a warning. He was by nature a very cruel man and a voice would sometimes warn him "Vengeance will come". But he shrugged his shoulders and ignored it.

He produced a son and heir and arranged a grand event to celebrate the birth, to which many dignitaries were invited. There was drinking, singing and dancing and one of those providing the entertainment was a harpist. A voice above the palace called out "Vengeance" but in the general noise of merrymaking only the harpist heard it. Suddenly the harpist spotted a bird which was beckoning him away from the palace. So he followed the bird, and after walking some distance began to regret leaving the palace and tried to find his way back alone. But, as it was dark, he soon lost his way and settled down to sleep on a hillside. When morning dawned he saw a large lake where the palace had stood and floating on it was his harp.

Today Llyn Tegid is one of the most popular natural attractions in Wales and is managed by the Snowdonia National Park.

But Borrow had little to say concerning the lake, being more interested in recording conversations with two men whom he met at the 'White Lion', a waiter, who revealed a great dislike of anything to do with Llangollen, and a commercial traveller selling drapery, who had been born in America of Welsh parents but had learned to speak the language fluently. This gave him the edge over his English counterparts who would have encountered difficulty in communicating with customers in nineteenth century Wales. Like Mr Jingle in Dickens' "The Pickwick Papers" the man spoke in curious, staccato sentences. When Borrow asked him whether the English travellers posed a competitive threat he exclaimed:

'English travellers! Don't know the language and nothing else. Could whip a dozen any day. Regularly flummax them'.

Walking up Stryd Fawr I reflected that I could not be anywhere else but in Wales. A Crosville bus drew to a stop to enable the extrovert driver to greet two friends on the pavement, a group of elderly men stood chatting together on a street corner, a grey-haired dog-collared man carrying a large Bible came out of one of the grocery shops; there was something distinctly Welsh about this scene in a town which has figured prominently in the historical life of Wales. The charismatic Methodist Thomas Charles established a Bala Preaching Festival, where sermons were delivered from dawn to dusk; Michael Jones was one of the founders of the Welsh colony in Patagonia; T.E. Ellis went to Westminster and was eventually appointed Gladstone's Chief whip; and R.J. Lloyd Price, a colourful local squire, distilled the first Welsh whiskey, virtually invented sheepdog trials and wrote a book with the delightful title "Tales My Dog Wagged".

Bala throws into relief the two extremes of the old and the new Wales. It is still a centre of the non-conformist tradition, an agricultural town where Welsh is spoken very widely. But is also has hotels and cafes which, out of economic necessity, make every effort to lure the tourist, while shops sell tourist artefacts of a kind to be found throughout North Wales. I should not be surprised if the Llyn Tegid monster now figures on T-shirts and mugs.

Is Teggie a creature of fact or fiction? Did he evolve uniquely in the depth of the lake or was he dreamed up by an enterprising publicist?

* * *

Back at Llangollen Borrow and his family decided to pay a visit to Chirk Castle. He was clearly extremely impressed by what he saw:

'...I thought of the many beauties who had been born in its chambers, had danced in its halls, had tripped across its court, and had subsequently given heirs to illustrious families'.

It has, over the centuries, been occupied by a number of important families – the Mortimers, the Mowbrays, the Beauchamps, the Beaufords, the Stanleys and the Middeltons. Earlier in this century it was owned by Lord Howard de Walden, an extremely wealthy patron of the arts.

The famous highly ornamented gates to the park were made by two local men, Robert and John Davies of Bersham.

Hundreds of visitors view the splendours of Chirk Castle each year, for it is now a National Trust property.

In 1854 the Crimean War was being wages on distant battlefields, and it figures in what Borrow wrote about his stay in Llangollen. As he walked back to the town from an excursion he heard

'...a sudden ringing of the bells of the place, and a loud shouting'.

It was thought that the British army had taken the important naval port of Sebastopol, and there was much excitement in the town as a result.

'...a wild running troop of boys was shouting "Sebastopol wedi cymmeryd. Hurrah! Hurray!" Old Mr Jones was standing bareheaded at his door. "Ah," said the old gentleman. "I am glad to see you. Let us congratulate each other. Sebastopol taken and in so short a time".'

But the celebrations are short lived for news followed of

'...disasters and disgrace on the part of the British; there was no more shouting at Llangollen in connection with the Crimean expedition...It was quite right and consistent with the justice of God that the British arms should be subjected to disaster and ignominy'.

The futility of war is inexplicable and one cannot be accused of pessimism in assuming that there will always be wars between conflicting factions. As I write senseless loss of life has taken place in Bosnia, and the IRA have resumed an insane bombing campaign.

* * *

While at Llangollen Borrow purchased a copy of a book entitled "Y Llwyn Celyn" ("The Holy Grove") which contained what he described, with delight, as

'...probably the most remarkable autobiography ever penned".

The author was Thomas Edwards, more popularly known as Twm o'r Nant, whom I have already mentioned briefly in the second chapter.

His life and work fascinated Borrow, and he devoted two entire chapters to Twm, writing at greater length about him than about any of the other national poets.

Twm o'r Nant was born near Llannefydd in 1738 in a dwelling on land which had once belonged to Iolo Goch. He attended school for a mere three weeks or so before taking up work as a farm labourer. According to one source he was introduced to the bardic tradition by fellow labourers in their leisure hours. Unable to afford the luxury of ink for his quill, he is reputed to have used elderberry juice instead. After his marriage he and his wife took a smallholding near Nantglyn and, apart from his agricultural work, he also earned money as a wood carter. When three of his horses died he was forced to make an even more determined effort at writing and he began work on his famous interlude plays. But eventually he fell into debt and was forced to leave North Wales in an effort to avoid his creditors. He settled in Llandeilo and kept a tavern there, as well as working as a toll-gate keeper. But eventually he did return to the Vale of Clwyd and lived in Denbigh. He continued his writing and turned his hand to a number of skills, including that of stonemasonry. He became well known for his feats of physical strength. Twm died in 1810 and was buried at Eglwys Wen in Denbigh and part of the inscription on the grave describes him as 'The Welsh Shakespeare'. One writer has suggested that a far more accurate comparison would be with the satirist Jonathan Swift.

A school and a community theatre in Denbigh both commemorate his name – Ysgol Twm o'r Nant and Theatr Twm o'r Nant.

There is a link of a kind between Twm and Bishop William Morgan, for a descendent of Morgan's, Arthur Jones, married a daughter of Twm's.

There is also an oblique link with the English poet Shelley. For a time Shelley stayed at a house called Tan Rallt at Tremadog, and it seems that at a later stage Twm's portrait hung in one of the rooms there.

Borrow's sentiments about Twm are summed up in these words:

'A time will come when interludes will cease to be read, but his making ink out of elderberries, his battle with the "cruel fighter". his teaching the horses to turn the crane, and his getting the ship to the water will be talked of in Wales till the peak of Snowdon shall fall down'.

A book on Welsh Methodism had just been published at Wrexham and Borrow wished to buy a copy, and so he decided to walk there.

'...I wished to explore the hill-road which led to Wrexham...If one wants to take any particular walk, it is always well to have some business, however trifling, to transact at the end of it...'

His desire to read the book reveals Borrow in a more mellow, and less prejudiced light than in most of the rest of the book.

On his way to Wrexham, a journey which as always he describes in a most interesting way, he got somewhat lost. After tramping through what appeared to be a virtual wilderness he saw

'...some small grimy-looking huts, which I suppose where those of colliers.'

Here we have his first reference to the industrialisation of Wales, a development which it would have been difficult for him to ignore at that time.

In this hut settlement he encountered a miner and it was not a convivial meeting. Borrow addressed him in Welsh but the man responded in English. Borrow obstinately continued in Welsh and the man took him to task in no uncertain terms for his failure to converse in the English tongue.

'Why, I never saw such a low, illiterate fellow in my life' the miner told him.

Reflecting on this salutary experience Borrow wrote:

'Here I had to pay for the over-praise which I lately received'.

As he approached Wrexham he saw

'...a strange looking house upon a slope on the right hand. It was very large, ruinous and seemingly deserted'.

Seeing a woman knitting at the door of a nearby cottage he asked her the name of the building and she informed that that it was called Cadogan Hall, and had the reputation of being haunted.

Having purchased his book at Wrexham Borrow then made his way to the Wynnstay Arms in the town in order to have dinner. The waiters, noticing the book, mistook him for a Baptist preacher.

'He has been preaching among the hills', exclaimed one to another, 'Don't you see his Bible.'

He fell into conversation with a commercial traveller and when he told this man of his intention to walk back to Llangollen that night the traveller was clearly alarmed:

'I would not go on foot there for fifty pounds'.
'Why not?' said I.
'For fear of being knocked down by colliers, who will be all out and drunk.'

Borrow, being something of a pugilist, said that he will be perfectly able to deal with such a situation:

'With this book I am sure I can knock down one, and I think I can find play for the other with my fists'.
The commercial traveller looked at me. 'A strange kind of Baptist minister,' I thought I heard him say.

When he reached Ruabon he heard

'...a prodigious noise in the public-houses...'

He was directed to take a short cut through some fields, and the description which follows is so striking that it deserves to be quoted fully:

I struck across the fields and should probably have tumbled half a dozen times over pales and the like, but for the light of the Cefn furnaces before me which cast their red glow upon my path. I debouched upon the Llangollen road near to the tramway leading to the collieries. Two enormous sheets of flame shot up high into the air from ovens, illumining two spectral chimneys as high as steeples, also smoky buildings, and grimy figures moving about. There was a clanging of engines, a noise of shovels and a falling of coals truly horrible. The glare was so great that I could distinctly see the minutest lines upon my hand. Advancing along the tramway I obtained a nearer view of the hellish buildings, the chimneys and the demoniac figures. It was just such a scene as one of those described by Ellis Wynn in his Vision of Hell.

The Welsh industrial landscape in the nineteenth century certainly did not go unnoticed by other literary tourists, but few descriptions rank with Borrow's for vividness and directness. One is reminded of a famous painting of Coalbrookdale, where flames are depicted shooting into the night sky while the figures of men labour at their exacting task below this inferno.

In late October Mrs Borrow and her daughter decided to leave for London, and Borrow intended to follow them there after completing his pedestrian tour. In preparation for his journey he tells us that

'I bought a small leather satchel with a lock and key, in which I placed a white linen shirt, a pair of worsted stockings, a razor and a prayer book...'

He was concerned about the fate of the church cat, which they were unable to take with them:

'...it would, of course, not do to leave it in the garden to the tender mercies of the Calvinistic Methodists of the neighbourhood...'

But, to his relief, he found

'...a young woman of sound Church principles'

who was prepared to give the cat a home.

Chapter Ten

SYCHARTH – LLANRHAEADR-YM-MOCHANT – PISTYLL RHAEADR – BALA AGAIN – DINAS MAWDDWY

The border region is one which has always fascinated me. This is partly because I have a good deal of border blood in my veins, both my father and mother having come from Montgomeryshire.

Along the hills of the marches kings and barons have fought to defend their territories, and the original boundary has been shifted over the centuries by historical forces. Offa's Dyke, running one hundred and seventy miles from South to North, reflects this, and does not correspond with the border line on today's maps. The Maelor district of the old county of Flint, for example, was once a part of England.

Offa was a king of Mercia who was more than a little anxious to put an end to the plunderings of the Welsh. There was a limit to the number of soldiers at his disposal at any one time and consequently stretches of the Dyke were not continually defended, which was of distinct advantage to the Welsh.

Today, of course, Offa's Dyke is a long distance footpath and it is the conservationists who are now involved in a battle, for the path is becoming seriously eroded in places under the pressure of the thousands of feet which tramp along it each year. But I wonder how many of these earnest walkers are aware of the rich historical and cultural heritage of the borders?

The region has figured prominently in literature, and the names of the poet A.E. Housman and the novelist Mary Webb spring immediately to mind. More recently the absorbing Brother Cadfael Medieval who-done-it novels of Ellis Peters have focused attention on the marcher country in a literary context.

But a Welsh-language poet who wrote of the region is Iolo Goch. Born in the Vale of Clwyd in about 1320 he was one of the first poets to write praise poems for the gentry, and enjoyed widespread patronage during his lifetime. One of his patrons was Owain Glyndŵr and he stayed with this great Welsh leader at his home, Sycharth.

Sycharth is situated near the village of Llangedwyn, but today you will look in vain for any trace of the structure of the building. What you will see is a hill in a field. Borrow described this as:

'...not an artificial hill but the work of nature, except that to a certain extent it has been modified by the hand of man'.

He goes on:

'On the top of this hill in a timber house dwelt the great Welshman Owain Glyndŵr, with his wife, a comely kindly woman, and his progeny, consisting of stout boys and blooming girls, and there he feasted bards who requited his hospitality with alliterative odes very difficult to compose...There he dwelt for many years, the virtual if not the nominal king of North Wales...'

Borrow then proceeds to give us his translation of Iolo Goch's tribute to Sycharth. However he is mistaken when he states that the poem was composed when the poet was 'upwards of a hundred years', for he probably died when he was about eighty.

Tis water girdled wide about
It shows a wide and stately door
Reached by a bridge the water o'er
Tis formed of buildings coupled fair,
Coupled is every couple there;
Within a quadrate structure tall,
Master the merry pleasures all.
Co-jointly are the angles bound –
No flaw in all the place is found.
Structures in contact meet the eye
Upon the hillocks top on high;
Into each other fastened they
The form of a hard knot display.
There dwells the chief we all extoll
In timber house on lightsome knoll

Upon four wooden columns proud
Each column thick and firmly bas'd
And upon each a loft is placed;
In these four lofts which coupled stand
Repose at night the minstrel band;
Four lofts they were in pristine state
But now, partitioned, form they eight.
Tiled is the roof, on each house top
Rise smoke-ejecting chimneys up
All of one form there are nine halls
Each with nine wardrobes within its walls
With linen white as well supplied
As fairest shops in famed Cheapside
Behold that church with cross upraised
And with its windows neatly glazed.
All houses are in this comprest –
An orchard's near it of the best.
Also a park where void of fear
Feed antlered herds of fallow deer.
A warren wide my chief can boast.
Of goodly steeds a countless host.
Meads where for hay the clover grows,
Cornfield which hedges trim enclose
A mill a rushing brook upon,
And pigeon tower fram'd of stone.
A fishpond deep and dark to see
To cast nets in when need there be
Which never yet was known to lack
A plenteous store of perch and jack
Of various plumage birds abound
Herons and peacocks haunt around
What luxury doth his hall adorn
Showing of cost a sovereign scorn
His ale from Shrewsbury town he brings.
His usquebagh is drink for kings;
Bragget he keeps, bread white of look
And, bless the mark, a bustling cook
His mansion is the minstrel's home
You'll find them there whene'er you come
Of all her sex his wife's the best;
The household through her care is blest;

She's scion of a knightly tree,
She's dignified, she's kind and free
His bairns approach me, pair by pair,
Oh what a nestful of chieftains there
Here difficult it is to catch
A sight of either bolt or latch
The porters place here none will fill;
Here largesse shall be lavished still
And ne'er shall thirst or hunger rude
In Sycharth venture to intrude.
A noble leader, Cambria's knight,
The lake possesses, his by right
And in that azure water placed
The castle by each pleasure grac'd.

But the English burned Sycharth to the ground in the fury and thrust of war. As I stood on the site of Sycharth reading this poem aloud to my wife, my mind was filled with speculative reflections.

Glyndŵr is a legend in the folk history of his country, a man with a firm vision of a Welsh independent state. Even the greatest English poet has payed tribute to him:

'In faith, he is a worthy gentleman,
Exceedingly well-read and profited
In strange concealments, valiant as a lion
And wondrous affable, and as bountiful
As mines in India'.

Gazing at the peaceful autumn countryside around Sycharth I thought of the present predicament of Wales, a country which central government still appears to regard as a colonial outpost. If it is at all possible to think in terms of a present day Glyndŵr as we approach the millennium then we certainly need one. In the realm of my imagination I have this image of a machiavellian manipulator who will wage an unrelenting struggle with the drab men in grey at Westminster and win the day for the Welsh nation.

But this is the stuff of sheer fantasy...

* * *

At Llansilin Borrow is mistaken for a South Walian at the local inn.

'How do you know that I come from South Wales' said I.
'By your English,' said the old fellow, 'anybody may know you are
South Welsh by your English; it is cursedly bad.'

The old man probably found Borrow's accent difficult to understand
because of his Norfolk origins. So he asks him to speak Welsh, but this
only serves to confirm the man's impression:

'...who but a South Walian would talk Welsh in that manner? It's
nearly as bad as your English'.

The unofficial ruler of that part of Wales in Victorian times was Sir
Watkin Williams Wynne and there are a number of references to him in
the pages of 'Wild Wales'. Poaching was rife and while enjoying his ale
Borrow is disturbed by

'...a rabble round of gamekeepers and river watchers'.

Among other things they declared their loyalty to Sir Watkin. But the old
man viewed them rather cynically.

'They are all from Wrexham, a mixture of broken housekeepers and
fellows too stupid to learn a trade; a set of scamps...They say they will
stand up for Sir Watkin, and so they will, but only in a box in the
court to give evidence. They won't fight for him on the banks of the
river'.

Accompanied by the innkeeper Borrow goes to view the grave of Huw
Morys at Llansilin Church. He pays homage to the bard in a dramatic,
some might say excessive way.

'...taking off my hat I went down on my knees and kissed the cold
slab covering the cold remains of the mighty Huw'.

Gazing at the church entrance he

'...remembered how many times Huw Morys had walked out of that
porch at the head of the congregation, the clergyman yielding his own
place to the inspired bard'.

As it was in Victorian times, Llansilin is still a peaceful and rather charming border community.

While walking around the village I stopped to pass the time of day with a short, dapper well dressed man of about sixty. He had a distinctive Montgomeryshire accent. After we had analysed the weather, as is the way with the Welsh, he asked me where I was from. When I told him he asked if I was staying in the Llansilin area, to which I explained that I was following Borrow's footsteps through North Wales. His eyes lit up.

'Do you know,' he exclaimed in an animated way, 'I think I've had more pleasure from old Borrow's book than from any other book I've read. He was quite a character wasn't he...'

'Yes he...' I tried to interject, but it was obvious that nothing would now stem his enthusiasm.

'Did you know he could speak Welsh as well as any Welshman...'

'Well he...'

'And of course he could speak other languages as well. They say he mastered Spanish...'

'That's right...'

'And then there were the gypsies, of course...'

'Of course...'

'There wasn't much he didn't know about the gypsies, you know...'

'Indeed, yes he was...'

'And he could walk many miles in one day. Did you know that?'

'Oh yes, I knew that' I replied.

The conversation must have continued in this way for some ten minutes, and I once again concluded that the majority of people like the sound of their own voices much more than other people's. As I walked on he gave me a hearty wave from the other end of the village street, and I raised my arm in a half wave.

* * *

The old counties of Denbighshire and Montgomeryshire, which disappeared in 1974, were divided at Llanrhaeadr-ym-Mochnant by the river Rhaeadr.

The village has a population of approximately nine hundred and fifty people and wears an air of well being. In one direction you travel ten miles in order to cross the border into England, but going in a westward direction you travel over the beautiful Berwyn to Bala.

It was at Llanrhaeadr that work was undertaken which determined the course of Welsh history and culture. I refer, of course, to William Morgan's translation into Welsh of both Testaments of the Bible in the later sixteenth century. His unstinting devotion to this labour of love, far from any centre of learning, had a profound influence on both the religious life of the nation, on its spoken language and on its literature.

It comes as a surprise, therefore, that in his account of Llanrhaeadr Borrow only includes an incidental reference to Morgan and even this is factually incorrect. While visiting the church he asks the clerk:

'Have any remarkable men been clergymen of this church?'

To which the clerk replied:

'Several, sir; amongst its vicars was Doctor William Morgan the great South Welshman...'

Borrow evidently knew little, if anything, concerning Morgan for, being the kind of person who would wish to take advantage in conversation, he would surely have corrected the clerk. Morgan, as every Welsh schoolboy knows, was, in fact, born at Penmachno in Dyffryn Conwy.

It is surprising in view of Borrow's passion for things Welsh, and his considerable interest in the language, that he should virtually ignore such a very important figure.

The contemporary Welsh-language poet James Nicholas sums up Morgan's achievement in one of his poems. I quote two stanzas from Tony Conran's translation:

All honour to Morgan's name!
Despite his troubles, William
Gave Wales the word of that age,
Gave, too, growth to the language
And, from what it was then, gave all
Its essence to survival.

Four centuries we counted –
O such work went into it!
God's word, open on the page,
A great saviour of the language.
On God's book, man's long labour:
Look at it – it's new once more!

My late father was a native of the Llanrhaeadr area, having been brought up on a smallholding. He was one of a family of fourteen and would sometimes tell me of the difficulties of life during the first world war period, the physical deprivations and the severe financial restraints. So, for this reason, if for no other, it is a place which I have a particular affection for.

* * *

Foaming and frothing from mountainous height,
Roaring like thunder the Rhaeadr falls;
Through its silvery splendour the eye may delight,
Its fury the heart of the bravest appals.

These are the words of an englyn on Pistyll Rhaeadr, which is one of the seven wonders of Wales. Six of these are situated in north east Wales and one – Wrexham steeple – has already been referred to.

In its spectacular fall from the Berwyn hills this cataract crashes over the sheer rocks for some 260 feet over a natural arch and into a deep basin.

'There are many remarkable cataracts in Britain and the neighbouring isles but this, the grand cataract of North Wales, far exceeds them all in altitude and beauty...I never saw water falling so gracefully, so much like beautiful threads as here.'

Today Pistyll Rhaeadr is very much on the tourist map and picnic tables can be found in the area. The sight of it is one which cannot fail to prompt a response from all who appreciate natural beauty, but, in terms of description, perhaps only a poet could do it justice.

* * *

From Llanrhaeadr Borrow was accompanied over the Berwyns to Bala by a guide. While striding through the hinterland the guide stopped on a few occasions to examine the heads of some of the sheep in order to ascertain whether they were infected by the pwd or moor disorder.

At this point Borrow revealed a knowledge of animal husbandry, recommending 'a decoction of hoarhound' for the malady.

'Pour some of this down the sheep's throat twice a day, by means of a horn, and the sheep will recover for the bitterness will destroy the worm...'

The small farms which existed in the hills in 1854 have over the years grown fewer and much larger. This has resulted in the depopulation of highland regions, creating vast ranches. All this is in the interest of a necessary productivity and efficiency in farming.

Having spent a stormy night at Bala's White Lion Borrow devoured an extremely large breakfast the following morning:

> 'What a breakfast! pot of hare; ditto of trout; pot of prepared shrimps; dish of plain shrimps; tin of sardines; beautiful beef-steak; eggs, muffin; large loaf and butter, not forgetting capital tea. There's a breakfast for you!'

Today, even if we were able to consume such a gargantuan feast, we would probably be inhibited from doing so either by the sheer cost of the foods included, the degree of cholesterol contained in them, or both.

Suitably refreshed he set out to attend a church service in the nearby village of Llanuwchllyn. Four years after Borrow's visit the writer and educationalist O.M. Edwards was born there. His work in making young people aware of the importance of their heritage has created for him a place in the modern history of Wales.

It was at Bala that our traveller reflected on the number of Joneses he had encountered

> '...that eternal name of Jones'.

Next to Borrow A.G. Bradley ranks as the most readable of the tourists who have written about Wales. When he visited Bala he concluded that

> '...if ever among the wonders the future has in store a great reunion of the Jones clan should be celebrated there is not the slightest doubt it should be held at Bala, though competition throughout North Wales would be keen enough'.

Rural Wales was indeed the wild country which the title of the book suggests and Borrow provides vivid descriptions of the landscape at certain points.

In the Mawddach area for example, he describes the isolation and harshness of the bare hills:

> '...Scenery of the wildest and most picturesque kind...hills were here; some tall and short, others huge and humpy; hills were on every side'.

Eventually he arrived at Cywarch:

'Aber Cywarch', I cried, springing half a yard into the air. 'Why that's the place where Ellis Wynn composed his immortal "Sleeping Bard".'

When he got to Dinas Mawddwy it was

'...little more than a collection of dirty huts. But though a dirty squalid place, I found it anything but silent and deserted'.

This was, in fact, a mining camp, for there was a fair amount of lead mining in north-west Wales in the nineteenth century. Here rough men are described as 'staggering about', by which I assume that Borrow meant that they were intoxicated. Many of them, he noted, had red hair and he assumed that they may have been descendants of the famous Red Bandits of Mawddwy. These were thieves and brigands who dwelt in the Mawddwy and Cwm Dugoed areas in the sixteenth century. Thomas Pennant, writing in 1778, claimed that eighty of them were executed by order of Judge Lewis Owain, the Sheriff of Merioneth. But revenge is often sweet to the lawless, and the judge himself was murdered while returning from an assize court in Welshpool. At Mallwyd an inn commemorates the notorious associations of the area with the bandits: The Brigand Inn. In Borrow's time the biggest lawbreakers would probably have been the numerous poachers from the region, stealthy men who perfected their skills on river banks in the dead of night or in the woodland areas before dawn. It is easy nowadays to romanticise their lifestyle, but one has to bear in mind that frequently poaching was carried out by poor people in order to provide food for their families and that the penalty, if one was caught, could be harsh indeed.

At an inn at Cemmaes Borrow was regarded with some suspicion. As he entered the place suddenly became silent and the other drinkers stared at him in a rather hostile manner. This feeling was increased when

'...I slowly and deliberately drew my note book out of my waistcoat pocket, unclasped it, and took my pencil from the loops at the side, and forthwith began to jot down observation upon the room and company...'

It was from such jottings and observations made in the summer and autumn of 1854 that 'Wild Wales' was eventually written, and we will leave our traveller as he sets out for mid and south Wales in search of further adventures.

I had reached the end of my own journey too, a literary pilgrimage on which I had travelled through some of the most beautiful scenery in the British isles.

I recalled the words of the poet Taliesin, quoted by Borrow:

Their lord they shall praise
Their language they shall keep,
Their land they shall lose
Except Wild Wales.

POSTSCRIPT

"Wild Wales" has gone into numerous editions over the years and within the last two years has been reprinted by a publishing company in Wales for the first time.

But we often forget that Borrow's intense interest in Wales and its people extends beyond the pages of this travel classic. A collection of his translations from the Welsh was edited by Ernest Rhys and appeared under the title "Welsh Poems and Ballads" in 1915, and in 1928 Herbert G. Wright edited his prose pieces about the history and literature of Wales under the title "Celtic Bards, Chiefs and Kings". He was responsible for making available to a wider readership that seminal work by Ellis Wynne "Gweledigaetheu y Bardd Cwsc" ('The Sleeping Bard'). Opinions concerning the quality of his translations differ among Welsh scholars, but this is a matter on which I am not qualified to venture a personal opinion.

But why, we may wonder, is Borrow's considerable interest in gypsy life not reflected in "Wild Wales", for he was, after all, the author of "The Romany Rye" and "Lavengro", and had compiled a dictionary of the Romany language.

Theodore Watts-Dunton, a contemporary of his, went as far as to claim that

'...it was eccentric to write a book upon Wales and to ignore so picturesque a feature as the Welsh gypsies'.

Borrow's exclusion of the gypsies of Wales is, therefore, inexplicable, especially when we recall the claim by Watts-Dunton that

'...beyond doubt the finest specimens of the Romany race are – or were – to be found in Wales'.

During his fairly prolonged visit one would have expected Borrow to have at least devoted a little space to them.

But to end on a much more positive note, the value of "Wild Wales" for today's reader surely rests partly, at least, outside the pages of the book. With the wisdom of hindsight we are made vividly aware, through this account of early-Victorian Wales, of the tremendous changes which have come about since then. Retrospectively everything is thrown into sharp relief.

In the final decade of the twentieth century, Wales remains a country of beautiful and varied landscapes, of a people who are proud of their history and culture, a land which still produces gifted poets.

George Borrow discovered "a land of old renown" and so it remains today.